Empower yoursel[f with the] **knowledge you nee**[d to] **cope with o**[bsessive compulsive] **disorder.**

Has your child been recently diagnosed with OCD, and you aren't sure how to move forward?

Do you suspect your child has OCD and are looking for advice on what signs to look out for?

Do you need guidance on how to parent a child with OCD?

Obsessive-Compulsive Disorder is a debilitating condition, especially for children who don't know whether what they are experiencing is normal or how to cope with intrusive thoughts and actions. This book will teach you and your child how to navigate this challenging journey.

In this book, you will:

- Explore OCD, including the symptoms and characteristics of childhood OCD.

- Get your questions about the origins, diagnosis, treatment, and potential outcomes answered.

- Learn how to recognize overpowering OCD symptoms, how they affect family relationships, and your child's ability to manage day-to-day life.

- Find strength in unity by learning how to rally against this unseen adversary, externalizing obsessive thoughts, and more.

- Gain a deeper understanding of the power of Exposure Response Prevention (ERP).

- Learn how your child's diet might affect their condition and what you can do to enhance the positive effects of the mind-gut connection.

- Master the art of creating a personal defense strategy for your child by assessing their needs, supporting them, and tracking their progress.

- Identify the best way to share your plan with your child to empower them.

- Understand how to address challenging responses and other setbacks on your child's road to recovery.

- Reveal the best strategies for navigating forward to ensure your child's continued progress.

By providing comprehensive information about childhood OCD and plenty of hands-on parental techniques, this book will help you and your child triumph over the trials and tribulations of their condition.

With the wealth of knowledge provided in this guide, you'll have all the tools you need to support and care for a child with OCD. You're not alone, and we will get through this together.

How to Help Your Child Thrive with OCD

A Parents All You Need to Know Guide to Help Children with Obsessive Compulsive Disorder

© **Copyright 2023 - All rights reserved.**

The content contained within this book may not be reproduced, duplicated, or transmitted without direct written permission from the author or the publisher.

Under no circumstances will any blame or legal responsibility be held against the publisher, or author, for any damages, reparation, or monetary loss due to the information contained within this book, either directly or indirectly.

Legal Notice:

This book is copyright protected. It is only for personal use. You cannot amend, distribute, sell, use, quote, or paraphrase any part of the content within this book without the consent of the author or publisher.

Disclaimer Notice:

Please note the information contained within this document is for educational and entertainment purposes only. All effort has been executed to present accurate, up-to-date, reliable, and complete information. No warranties of any kind are declared or implied. Readers acknowledge that the author is not engaging in the rendering of legal, financial, medical, or professional advice. The content within this book has been derived from various sources. Please consult a licensed professional before attempting any techniques outlined in this book.

By reading this document, the reader agrees that under no circumstances is the author responsible for any losses, direct or indirect, that are incurred as a result of the use of the information contained within this document, including, but not limited to, errors, omissions, or inaccuracies.

Table of Content

Introduction

Chapter 1: Decoding the Enigma

The Basics of OCD

Childhood vs. Adult OCD

Spotting the Signs

Case Study

Chapter Takeaways

Chapter 2: Parental Pulse

The Origins of OCD

The Diagnostic Journey

How Professionals Identify OCD in Children

Potential Outcomes

Chapter Takeaways

Chapter 3: Shadows in the Home

Recognizing Overpowering OCD

Ripple Effects

Managing Daily Life

The Martins - A Family's Disruption and Unity

Chapter Takeaways

Chapter 4: Strength in Unity

Rallying against the Unseen Adversary

Externalizing OCD

Refocusing Attention

The Role of Therapy

Chapter Takeaways

Chapter 5: Guiding Light

What Is ERP?

Key Components of ERP

Why ERP Is Effective

The Power of Exposure Response Prevention (ERP)

Success Stories

Chapter Takeaways

Chapter 6: The Mind-Gut Connection

Probiotics and Mental Health

Magnesium and Mental Health

Benefits of the Anti-inflammatory Diet

Sample Meals on the Anti-inflammatory Diet

Success Stories on the Anti-inflammatory Diet

Chapter Takeaways

Chapter 7: Assembling Your Arsenal

Addressing the Body Symptoms

Addressing the Thoughts Component

Dealing with the OCD Behavior Component

Building a Support System

Chapter Takeaways

Chapter 8: A Compassionate Confrontation

Sharing the Plan with Your Child

Ways to Discuss OCD

Why Your Child Might Resist

Normalizing Their Feelings of Discomfort

Setting Realistic Goals

Celebrating Achievements

Chapter Takeaways

Chapter 9: Braving the Storm

Addressing Difficult Responses

Emotional Outbursts

Why Emotional Outbursts Happen and How to Respond

Navigating Setbacks

Strategies to Regain Momentum

Coping with Intrusive Thoughts

Chapter Takeaways

Chapter 10: Navigating Forward

Preparing for Tomorrow

Maintaining Momentum

Ensuring Continued Progress Post Treatment

Preparing for Adulthood

Transitioning to Teen and Adult Years

Finding Support Groups

Types of OCD Support Groups

Questions to Ask the Moderator

Building a Community for Continued Success

Chapter Takeaways

Conclusion

References

Introduction

OCD is a mental illness that can be incredibly challenging for those without the right support and coping mechanisms. However, your child can lead a happy, fulfilling life with proper treatment, and coping strategies in place. Getting started early is crucial to helping your child manage this disorder effectively.

You and your child might have already made efforts to combat OCD, but logical approaches don't always work well against this nonsensical condition. If you're like most families dealing with OCD, you might be feeling confused and frustrated because you don't know where to turn for help.

This book will provide you with guidance on how to recognize and treat OCD symptoms in your child. It's a manual on how to create a loving and supportive environment where your child can thrive. Most importantly, it will empower you to take an active role in your child's treatment and well-being. You are not powerless; you have the tools to positively impact your child's life. Don't worry if you can't find all the information you need elsewhere; this book has got you covered.

Keep in mind that while this book provides valuable tools and coping strategies, it cannot completely replace skilled therapy from an expert clinician. If you do need more assistance, working with a mental health professional who specializes in child anxiety and OCD may be the best course of action.

Chapter 1: Decoding the Enigma

"OCD is like having a bully stuck inside your head, and nobody else can see it." — Krissy McDermott

Imagine a bully always standing over you. Their threatening gaze follows you wherever you go as they bark out demands to do or say things that are either inappropriate for the situation or excessive. This is how children with Obsessive-Compulsive Disorder (OCD) can feel most of the time. They experience repeated emotions, thoughts, and visual images and because these are unwanted, they try to control them through compulsive behaviors. However, because the experience continues, the compulsions only bring temporary relief. Still, children with OCD feel compelled to repeat the actions because if they resist, they're brought into an emotional rollercoaster laced with severe anxiety.

It's a common misconception that people with OCD simply love to repeat behaviors like motion and words or excessive cleaning. While OCD has several forms, the experience is frightening, especially for children. As they grow older, children begin to feel the burden of their condition, accompanied by the notion that they aren't like most people and won't be accepted by others. This introductory chapter takes a deep dive into the fundamentals of OCD, including the causes, symptoms, and key differences between children and adults suffering from this condition.

The Basics of OCD

To give you an overview of OCD, you must familiarize yourself with its nature. Mental health professionals previously classified OCD as an anxiety disorder, given that it's the prevailing emotion sufferers experience. Nowadays, it's widely accepted that anxiety is only one key aspect of the disorder. The underlying cause leads to a wide array of other symptoms, including obsessive and intrusive thoughts and compulsive behavior.

Obsessive and intrusive thoughts and compulsive behavior are the two main symptoms of OCD. Everyone has irrational fears or ideas that seem outlandish and have no basis at all from time to time. However, with OCD, the obsessions can be constant and simply won't go away, no matter how hard a person tries to ignore them. The more someone tries to push these beliefs into the back of their mind, the more distress they cause. For example, a person might worry that they'll catch a terrifying disease or humiliate themselves by acting inappropriately in a certain situation. Or they might live in constant fear that their loved ones will get hurt. While some of these ideas are less disruptive, they'll still cause discomfort. Other thoughts, however, can make it challenging for a person to function on a day-to-day basis.

Each obsession is followed by a compulsive action, which a person feels they must carry out repeatedly. For example, a person terrified of catching a disease will wash their hands regularly or clean every part of their home repeatedly. Those afraid of their loved ones getting hurt will continuously keep checking on friends and family to make sure everyone is ok. Like obsessions, compulsions are long-lasting and often negatively affect a person's life. They can't be ignored either. Otherwise, the compulsion to act on them comes back stronger, causing even more negative thoughts and feelings.

Those with OCD often spend several hours either mulling over their obsessive thoughts or engaging in a behavior that brings temporary relief from the anxiety caused by those intrusive ideas. They might even fail to realize how much time they spend trying to keep their obsessions in check or how this affects their lives, health, and well-being. For example, a cleanliness-obsessed individual can uncontrollably wash their hands until they start bleeding.

In some cases, a person will only experience obsessions or compulsions and not both. For instance, a person might have excessive thoughts about wanting to hurt someone, but they won't be compelled to control the feelings caused by their ideas. Or a person might engage in compulsive behavior without having obsessive thoughts beforehand. The crux of the matter is that whichever symptoms they have diminishes their quality of life.

Childhood vs. Adult OCD

While the symptoms of OCD are similar in adults and children, OCD in children can be more challenging to recognize for numerous reasons. Children can lack awareness of their thoughts and feelings, so they might not even realize that their experiences are unordinary and need to be addressed. In other words, they won't ask for assistance because they don't know they need it. Many children have symptoms for several years before being diagnosed by a mental health professional. At first, their symptoms might not be severe enough (even for parents or guardians) to notice. It might start with the constant need to stay beside a parent and gradually transform into an overwhelming fear that something terrible will happen to the parent when the child is not with them. The types of obsessions and compulsions children experience can also change over time. Symptoms generally worsen when a person experiences chronic stress. Due to a traumatic event, childhood OCD can quickly transform from a mild nuance into a condition so severe and time-consuming that it becomes disabling.

Obsessive thoughts in children can be mistaken for symptoms of other conditions, like Attention-Deficit/Hyperactivity Disorder (ADHD). This happens when the children's obsessive thoughts and compulsive behaviors begin to interfere with their learning and education.

A pivotal difference between childhood and adult OCD is seen in the compulsive behaviors and rituals children engage in. If a child is obsessed with an idea and has compulsive actions to deal with it, everyone around them must follow suit. For example, a child will refuse to sleep until a parent helps them check that everything and everyone is safe in the house. Or, they'll ask everyone to engage in the same excessive cleaning ritual they feel compelled to do before mealtime. Known as family accommodation behaviors, these actions are linked to extreme childhood OCD. While accommodating these needs makes it more challenging to cease engaging in compulsive behavior, friends and family might feel the need to perform the actions because they think this is what a child needs to feel better. You might think, if accommodating your child will relieve their distress, why not do as they ask? However, by doing so, you're only reinforcing their symptoms.

Childhood OCD is usually accompanied by conditions like tic disorders, ADHD, and other anxiety or neurodevelopmental disorders. Parts of this can be found in the genetic component of OCD. The same genes that contribute to childhood-onset OCD can raise the likelihood of the abovementioned comorbidities. Moreover, if a person is diagnosed with OCD as a child, their children are more likely to inherit the condition than if they were diagnosed as an adult.

Several conditions lead to the sudden development of OCD in kids and do not affect adults. For example, children ages 4-10 suffering from Pediatric Acute-Onset Neuropsychiatric Disorder (PANS) or Pediatric

Autoimmune Neuropsychiatric Disorder Associated with Streptococcal Infections (PANDAS) will be more likely to experience the acute onset of OCD symptoms.

Spotting the Signs

Going through phases of repetitive habits and actions is a normal part of childhood development. Many children love to arrange their toys in a specific way or put on only a particular combination of clothes. This is normal, even if it becomes a short-lived obsession (which is possible if they are undergoing change or stress). However, you need to be aware that your child may start experiencing distressing ideas alongside the repetitive behavior - especially if they can't control their urges to act on these thoughts.

OCD has three fundamental elements:

- **Obsessions**: Undesirable, invasive, and often repulsive images, urges, and thoughts suddenly flood the mind.

- **Feelings**: The obsessive thoughts induce a state of distress or severe anxiety.

- **Compulsions**: Due to their distress and anxiety, the child is driven to repetitive actions (or at least their mind is filled with thoughts of acting on them).

Compulsive behavior might relieve the dread for the time being, but this isn't always the case. Even if it does, the thoughts are bound to reemerge (along with the distress), and the child is caught in a vicious cycle.

Most children with OCD incur compulsions and obsessions, but either component can be less pronounced at times.

Obsessions

Have you ever left your house or were preparing for bed and thought to yourself, "Did I forget to lock the door?" Or maybe you were in a situation where you were upset about something, and your mind suddenly filled with intrusive and vivid mental thoughts or images? It happens to us all. However, if your child has regular ideas of potentially violent or unusual actions in their mind, they could be experiencing obsessions.

Typical obsessions in children with OCD include but aren't limited to the following:

- **Concern of intentionally hurting themselves or others** – for example, they might be afraid that they will strike someone else, like parents, siblings, or friends.

- **Worry about causing harm to themselves or others by misstep** – for instance, they might be afraid of flooding the house by letting the sink overflow.
- **Fear of catching an infection or disease** - by getting exposed to dirt, germs, and other unpleasant substances.
- **Getting fixated on order or symmetry** – for example, they might feel the need to check whether all their school material is arranged the same way while they are doing their homework.
- Feelings of discomfort if things aren't in the right place.
- Thoughts of doing something forbidden.
- Fear of losing their things, like their favorite toy, a keychain, etc.
- Violent and frightening mental pictures.
- Thoughts that tell them to check if everyone and everything around them is all ok.

While many people (children and adults) experience these thoughts, they won't last long, and their thoughts have no impact on their daily lives. The beliefs are classified as OCD-related obsessions if they induce distress or impede normal life functions like going to school, playing with friends, etc.

Compulsions

Compulsive behavior starts as a child's attempt to relieve or stop the uneasiness brought forth by obsessive ideas. However, this behavior is either disproportionate or, more often, not even connected to the original belief. For instance, a child might view even numbers as good and odd ones as bad, compulsively "replacing" the bad numbers with good ones (instead of 1 or 3 pieces of fruit, they must always take 2 or 4, etc.). Other children would compulsively count floor tiles while walking just to occupy their minds, while a third group might count because it simply feels right to them.

Typical compulsions include the following:

- Excessive hand washing and cleaning of all surfaces they touch.
- Checking to ensure safety, like checking if the doors are locked.
- Counting and recounting.
- Re-doing previously completed actions to ensure they are done correctly.

- Repeatedly arranging and reorganizing to satisfy a specific need.
- Accumulating things they don't need and use (hoarding).
- Constantly requesting reassurance from an adult.
- Chanting words out loud or in their mind.
- Thinking thoughts, they believe will cancel out the intrusive ideas.
- Avoiding situations, places, and people that trigger intrusive ideas.
- Checking rituals to make sure everything is where it needs to be.
- Repeatedly tapping or touching things.

Not all compulsions are as noticeable, so you'll need to pay attention to your child's behavior to spot the signs. Children experience temporary relief after engaging in a compulsive activity.

Case Study

Jenny's Story - From First Signs to Diagnosis

My daughter Jenny is eleven years old and suffers from obsessive-compulsive disorder. It all started when she was around six years old. I had no idea what was happening because I had heard little about OCD until then. When she was six, Jenny started developing a lot of unusual habits. One of them was adding "I think" before everything she said - whether it was her own thoughts or something she heard others say. At first, I found it amusing, but soon, it was making everyone in the family crazy. Not only that, but Jenny's friends started to tease her about it, as well. I asked her to stop saying it, telling her to pause before she started speaking to ensure she didn't begin with the phrase. However, I soon realized that she had no control over it. When I asked her to stop, she started crying and said she couldn't.

Another habit she developed is checking the lights and doors and worrying about whether the water is shut off in the bathroom. She would ask me to check these things with or for her all the time. Then, she started to worry if I was all right while away at work. She insisted I come to her room even if I arrived home very late when she was supposed to be sleeping. However, she couldn't sleep until she saw me. Her mind couldn't stop racing with worries. Sometimes, she would come to me and ask me *to sit with her on the couch and tap her knees with her hand repeatedly.*

At first, I thought she would outgrow these behaviors. One day, she told me that every time she exits the house, she has to imagine the number 3 in front of her and say, "Don't worry." to herself. She said these words are always on her mind. If she tries to redirect her thoughts and think of something nice, she becomes so afraid she feels like her chest wants to explode. She also told me that sometimes she fears that anything she does will result in something terrible occurring to someone she loves. She can't go to sleep before looking under her bed and out the window. She also must close her bedroom door three times and switch the nightlights on and off three times. I think this was the moment when I realized she needed professional help because things were getting worse.

After consulting with Jenny's pediatrician, I found a doctor specializing in treating children with obsessive thoughts and behaviors. She suspected Jenny had Obsessive-Compulsive Disorder and explained what this condition was. At first, I was terrified because I learned it was a lifelong condition - but at least we had a possible answer to what was wrong with my daughter. To diagnose Jenny, the doctor did a series of tests and gave her a few assignments to complete. For example, she asked Jenny to draw or write whenever she felt worries arising to see whether being engaged in something would keep her mind off the worries. She was to write and draw every day after school. When we went back for a checkup, Jenny said that when she does her writing and art, she doesn't worry about things so much. She keeps busy with it, so she doesn't have time to think about anything else. The doctor then officially diagnosed Jenny (she was almost eight at the time) with OCD and set out to determine the best treatment for her.

The doctor had a solid reputation for helping children with OCD and turned out to be the right choice because she was able to show Jenny the ways to push back her worries. The doctor encouraged Jenny to give each "worry" a funny name so that when she has them, the funny name will pop into her mind, making her smile and instantly relieving her of her worries. We practiced this a lot at home, too, and Jenny's worries started to go away. The doctor also helped me get in touch with support groups, where we met other children with OCD. Jenny found it much easier to bond with children who also have unwanted thoughts because she didn't feel judged.

Now that she is eleven, Jenny's OCD has gotten much better. She can talk about it more openly and says that on a lot of days, she doesn't even feel like she has OCD. I am very glad she got diagnosed. Now, she can learn how to tell her habits to go away. I just wish I acted earlier and asked for help sooner. Still, the diagnosis was a blessing because now Jenny has a chance of getting better and leading a normal life. She might struggle for a while, but, in the end, everything will be alright. - Kathleen

After they turn two, children begin to rely on structured schedules. They thrive on regular bedtime, mealtime, and bathing routines as this helps them make sense of their world. By the age of six, children develop group rituals (for playing games with rules and rhymes). Older children develop a hobby of collecting objects and might become preoccupied with it. All these ritualized behaviors are normal. They foster socialization and self-regulation skills, teaching children to cope with anxiety. However, when these are preceded by obsessive thoughts that become so frequent or the rituals become so intense that they interfere with one or more aspects of their lives, it is time to ask for professional help as they might be struggling with OCD.

Chapter Takeaways

- Obsessive-compulsive disorder (OCD) is a condition involving repeated sensory experiences, making the sufferer engage in compulsory actions and behaviors.

- OCD in children and adults manifests differently as children have less control over their thoughts, feelings, and behavior. Moreover, the symptoms are often mistaken for the signs of other conditions.

- The symptoms vary in intensity - some children only have one specific obsession-compulsion pair that does not affect their life, while others have several disruptive fear-action pairings.

- Fear that everything isn't okay, that things aren't in the right order, or they might get dirty or lost - accompanied by the compulsion of needing to double-check everything either by counting, cleaning, or inspecting - are the most common symptoms of OCD in children.

- Obsessions and compulsions are accompanied by a third symptom - extreme emotional experiences. Children can't stop the intrusive thoughts, and refraining from the action makes them anxious - both of which lead to profound distress.

- The two prominent symptoms of the condition (obsessions and compulsions) serve as a diagnostic tool for mental health professionals.

The next chapter takes an in-depth look at the background and diagnosis of OCD.

Chapter 2: Parental Pulse

"Name your differences with pride." – Dr Lucy Russell

Obsessive-Compulsive Disorder (OCD) is a complex mental health condition involving a combination of factors revolving around genetics, neurology, psychology, and the environment. While the exact cause of OCD is still incomprehensible, researchers have identified several distinct key factors that contribute to its development. This chapter will answer parents' burning questions about OCD and introduce treatment options.

The Origins of OCD

Genetics

Family History: Children with a family history of OCD are at a higher risk of developing the disorder. This evident link shows the genetics involved in OCD. However, note that having a family history does not guarantee someone will develop OCD, as a collective of several other factors are at play during the development of OCD.

Twin Studies: Several studies conducted on identical twins further support the involvement of genetics in OCD. Identical twins having the same genetic makeup can both develop OCD if one twin is already suffering from the condition. However, non-identical twins that only have 50% identical genes were found to be less likely to develop the condition.

Specific Genes: While researchers can still not pinpoint the genes involved in developing OCD, they have detected genes that increase the risk of developing OCD. These genes are often related to the regulation of neurotransmitters like serotonin, which is known to influence mood and anxiety disorders.

Environment

Stressful Life Events: Traumatic or stressful life events, like abuse, loss of a loved one, or significant life changes, can trigger the onset or worsening of OCD symptoms. These stressors become much more effective if the genetic makeup already shows an increased likelihood of developing OCD.

Childhood Experiences: Every childhood experience, especially negative experiences, has a profound effect on a child's mental well-being. Negative experiences can trigger the development of OCD. Likewise, facing neglect from parents and family members can contribute to developing anxiety disorders, including OCD, later in life.

Psychological Factors

Cognitive Patterns: Children with OCD develop specific cognitive patterns like having intrusive thoughts (obsessions) and having a staunch belief that engaging in certain behaviors (compulsions) will alleviate their anxiety. Obsessions are simply recurrent and uncontrollable urges and thoughts, whereas compulsions include behaviors like repetitive hand washing and repeatedly checking doors or mental acts like counting. The child feels driven to perform in response to the obsessions or according to rigid rules.

The urge to repeat these obsessions and compulsions is what fuels OCD. Cognitive-behavioral therapy (CBT) and exposure and response prevention (ERP) can help children identify and break free from these thought patterns.

Coping Mechanisms: During OCD, anxiety and stress go through the roof. These compulsive behaviors and obsessive thoughts develop as a way to cope with anxiety or distress. These behaviors, while initially providing relief, lead to the development of OCD.

Personality Traits: Every child develops certain personality traits that differ from their peers, like perfectionism and struggling with an excessive need for control. These traits may increase susceptibility to OCD as they can contribute to obsessions and compulsions centered around orderliness and cleanliness.

Brain Structure and Function

Neurological Circuits: Neuroimaging studies have revealed that children with OCD have abnormal activity in specific brain circuits, including the cortico-striato-thalamo-cortical (CSTC) circuit. This circuit is responsible for regulating thoughts, behaviors, and emotions. Dysfunction in these circuits can lead to the persistence of obsessions and compulsions.

Brain Regions: Abnormalities in specific brain regions, like the orbitofrontal cortex and the basal ganglia, are linked with the development of OCD. The orbitofrontal cortex is involved in decision-making and emotional processing, while the basal ganglia affects motor control and habit formation.

OCD is a complex and multifaceted disorder typically arising from the interplay of these genetic, environmental, psychological, and neurological factors. Additionally, individual experiences and the specific nature of obsessions and compulsions can vary widely. Effective treatment involves a combination of therapies (such as CBT) and, in some cases, medication to manage symptoms and improve overall quality of life.

The Diagnostic Journey

Identifying Obsessive-Compulsive Disorder (OCD) in children can be challenging, as children don't always express their thoughts and feelings clearly. Some levels of obsessional thinking and compulsive behavior is typical in childhood development. However, when these behaviors become excessive, distressing, and interfere with a child's daily life, it could indicate OCD. A mental health professional will identify OCD in children with the following assessments:

Clinical Assessment: The process begins with a clinical assessment conducted by a mental health professional, such as a pediatrician, child psychologist, or child psychiatrist. This assessment may include the following components:

Interviews: The child and their parents or caregivers are interviewed to gather information about their behavior, emotions, and specific concerns or symptoms.

Behavioral Observation: The child's behavior is evaluated for signs of distress or unusual behaviors during the assessment.

Medical History: Detailed medical history is obtained to rule out any medical conditions or medications contributing to the symptoms.

Diagnostic Criteria: There are established criteria to diagnose OCD in children, known as the Statistical Manual of Mental Disorders (DSM-5). According to these criteria, compulsions and obsessive thoughts manifest in distress or impaired brain functioning, both as potential risk factors for developing OCD.

Questionnaires: The symptoms of OCD in children are further evaluated through questionnaires and are designed to reveal the severity and impact of the present symptoms on the child.

Developmental Considerations: The child's age and developmental stage are considered when diagnosing OCD. Younger children have a harder time articulating their thoughts and feelings, so assessment methods are adapted accordingly.

Differential Diagnosis: Most mental health illnesses like generalized anxiety disorder, specific phobias, or attention-deficit/hyperactivity disorder (ADHD) have symptoms similar to OCD. Professionals will carefully differentiate between these disorders to make an accurate diagnosis.

Duration and Functional Impact: A mental health professional will assess the symptoms' duration and functional impact. Suppose compulsive behaviors and obsessive thoughts interfere with the child's daily life, academics, social, and family functioning and are evident for more than one hour a day. Mental health professionals will state this indicates the development of OCD.

Family History: Professionals may inquire about the family's history of mental health conditions, as OCD can run in families.

Collateral Information: Information from multiple sources, such as teachers or other caregivers, is gathered to provide a more comprehensive understanding of the child's behavior and symptoms.

Cultural Considerations: Professionals will also consider cultural factors when assessing for OCD, as cultural norms and beliefs can influence the presentation of symptoms.

Once an OCD diagnosis is established, the child and their family work with mental health professionals to develop an appropriate treatment plan. This will include a combination of therapies like CBT, ERP, and, in some cases, medication to manage symptoms. Early diagnosis and intervention are crucial in helping children with OCD lead healthier and more fulfilling lives.

How Professionals Identify OCD in Children

Cognitive-Behavioral Therapy (CBT)

Exposure and Response Prevention (ERP): ERP is the cornerstone of CBT for OCD. It involves systematically and gradually exposing children to the situations, thoughts, or objects that trigger their obsessions. During these exposures, they are explicitly instructed to refrain from engaging in their usual compulsive behaviors or rituals. For example, if someone has contamination obsessions and compulsions, they might be exposed to a mildly dirty object (exposure) and prevented from washing their hands (response prevention).

Hierarchy: ERP is structured in a hierarchy where the initial exposure is less anxiety-provoking but gradually becomes more challenging, allowing those affected to develop confidence and better handle their triggers.

Imaginal Exposure: In some cases, ERP involves imaginal exposure, where individuals vividly imagine the feared situation or thought without engaging in the compulsion.

Cognitive Restructuring: This therapy component can identify and challenge irrational or distorted thoughts associated with their obsessions. Taking these negative thoughts head-on encourages children to develop a rational and realistic perspective.

Homework: Assignments are given as part of therapy, including cognitive restructuring exercises and exposure-related activities.

Self-Monitoring: During the therapy, it's beneficial to keep a journal or diary to track obsessions, compulsions, and their associated anxiety levels as it helps map out progress.

Role of the Therapist: The therapist plays a pivotal role in guiding individuals through ERP, providing support, and helping them develop strategies to address their resisting compulsions.

Efficacy of CBT (ERP): ERP is highly effective for those with OCD, with numerous studies demonstrating significant symptom reduction. Improvement can be gradual, and it may take several months of consistent therapy to see substantial gains. Success rates vary, but many children experience marked improvement or remission of their symptoms.

Medication

Selective Serotonin Reuptake Inhibitors (SSRIs): These medications are used to treat OCD as they increase the level of serotonin, a neurotransmitter associated with mood regulation. Some SSRIs used to treat OCD include fluoxetine, sertraline, and fluvoxamine. These are prescription drugs the therapist prescribes after extensive evaluation of symptoms and their severity. The dosage varies according to the condition.

Efficacy of Medication: SSRIs are generally effective in reducing OCD symptoms, but their efficacy can vary. Efficacy is the ability of a medication to produce the desired outcomes. Some children might be unresponsive to a medication, whereas others might experience side effects limiting their use.

Side Effects: Common side effects of SSRIs include nausea, weight gain, dizziness, loss of appetite, lethargy, or agitation. If you find your child suffering from any of these side effects after taking the medication, it's best to discuss them with their healthcare provider.

Supportive Therapy

Psychoeducation: The first step is to educate parents and caregivers about OCD, its causes, and available treatments that are essential to supportive therapy.

Coping Strategies: Therapists will work with their patients to develop coping strategies for dealing with OCD symptoms and managing stress.

Support Groups: Participation in support groups can offer a sense of community and the opportunity to share experiences and coping strategies with others facing similar challenges.

Efficacy of Supportive Therapy: While not a primary treatment for OCD, supportive therapy is valuable in conjunction with CBT and medication. It provides emotional support, education, and practical tools for managing daily life with OCD.

Keep in mind that the effectiveness of treatments varies from person to person, and the choice of treatment should be tailored to the individual's specific symptoms and needs. Additionally, early intervention and ongoing support are key to improving the long-term prognosis for individuals with OCD. Consult with a mental health professional as soon as you notice OCD symptoms in your child to determine the most appropriate treatment plan.

Potential Outcomes

Early Intervention and Treatment

Excellent Outcome: When children with OCD receive prompt diagnoses and effective treatment, such as cognitive-behavioral therapy (CBT) with exposure and response prevention (ERP) or medication, many of their OCD symptoms significantly improve or even go into complete remission.

Normalization of Life: With successful treatment, children can experience normal daily lives. They can engage in typical activities, such as attending school, participating in extracurricular activities, and forming healthy friendships without the interference of OCD symptoms.

Maintenance Strategies: After achieving a positive outcome, children should continue to engage in maintenance strategies, such as periodic check-ins with a therapist or medication management, to prevent relapse.

Treatment Resistance

Partial Response: In some cases, children may not achieve full remission but experience a partial response to treatment. In other words, their OCD symptoms improve but do not disappear entirely. However, these improvements can still lead to a significantly better quality of life.

Functional Gains: Even with a partial response, children may regain the ability to function more effectively in their daily lives. They will learn to manage their symptoms and engage in age-appropriate activities.

Co-occurring Disorders

Co-occurring Conditions: Many children with OCD also experience co-occurring conditions, such as depression, anxiety disorders, or attention-deficit/hyperactivity disorder (ADHD). The presence of these additional conditions can complicate the treatment process.

Integrated Treatment: Managing co-occurring conditions involves an integrated treatment approach. Mental health professionals may address both OCD and the co-occurring disorders simultaneously to improve overall outcomes.

Resilience and Coping

Enhanced Coping Skills: Through treatment and support, children with OCD develop enhanced coping skills. These skills are invaluable not only for managing OCD symptoms but also for navigating life's challenges and stresses.

Growth and Development: Over time, children develop resilience, learning how to adapt to stressors and setbacks while maintaining their overall well-being.

Relapse Prevention

Relapse Risk: Even after successful treatment, there is a risk of relapse in some cases. Factors such as stress, major life changes, or treatment discontinuation can contribute to relapse.

Continued Support: Ongoing monitoring, follow-up appointments, and the use of relapse prevention strategies will minimize the risk of OCD symptom recurrence.

Quality of Life

Improved Quality of Life: Effective treatment enhances the quality of life for OCD patients and their families. As symptoms improve or remit, children can enjoy a more typical childhood experience, pursuing their interests, engaging in academic and extracurricular activities, and forming positive relationships.

Family Dynamics: Improved outcomes also positively impact family dynamics, reducing the stress and disruption that OCD symptoms bring to the household.

The prognosis for children with OCD varies based on factors like early intervention, treatment response, co-occurring conditions, and the severity of symptoms. While many experience substantial improvement or remission of their symptoms with appropriate treatment and support, others may face greater challenges.

Nevertheless, ongoing care, resilience, and coping skills can contribute to better outcomes and improved quality of life for children with OCD. Tailored treatment plans and close collaboration with mental health professionals are essential for achieving the best possible outcomes.

Chapter Takeaways

OCD Overview

- OCD is a mental health condition associated with distressing thoughts (obsessions) and repetitive behaviors (compulsions). These obsessions and compulsions are developed as a natural defense mechanism to alleviate anxiety but can intensify, leading to OCD.

Factors Contributing to OCD

- Brain abnormalities, genetics, and the environment are three main factors that contribute to the development of OCD.

Common Treatments for OCD

- Cognitive-behavioral therapy (CBT), particularly Exposure and Response Prevention (ERP), is a highly effective treatment for OCD.

- Medications, such as SSRIs, are used to manage symptoms.

- Supportive therapy, psycho-education, and support groups can complement primary treatments.

Prognosis for Children with OCD

- Early intervention and treatment greatly improve the prognosis for children with OCD.

- Many children respond well to treatment and can achieve symptom reduction or remission.

- Co-occurring conditions, such as depression or anxiety disorders, can impact treatment outcomes.
- Enhanced coping skills and resilience can benefit children with OCD.
- Ongoing monitoring and relapse prevention strategies are crucial.
- Improved quality of life is a common outcome with effective treatment and support.

Individualized Treatment

- Treatment plans should be tailored to the specific needs and symptoms of each child.
- A multidisciplinary approach involving mental health professionals, educators, and family support is often necessary.

The next chapter will help you understand how OCD affects everyone in the home and what you can do to prevent it from consuming the household.

Chapter 3: Shadows in the Home

"Family is supposed to be our safe haven, but very often it is the place where we find the deepest heartaches." – Iyanla Vanzant

OCD does not only affect the person who lives with the disorder. Families often carry a large portion of the distress that the illness causes. The nature of OCD is disruptive. Obsessions, compulsions, and rituals can detour the lives of an entire family. Simple activities like getting ready in the morning or going out on a family trip can quickly devolve into a nightmare. Additional education is needed to create a safe and productive home environment for families who have children experiencing OCD. The disorder does not have to hold your family back from living a fulfilled life, but there will inevitably be constraints that you need to function within. Raising children is already a complex task that takes years of commitment; OCD just adds to the list of concerns. However, OCD can be managed to ensure that each family member has their needs met in a functional household.

Recognizing Overpowering OCD

OCD can easily overthrow the kingdom of your home if it is allowed to run rampant. Many parents of children with OCD make the mistake of entertaining and participating in their child's compulsions or obsessions. This kind of enabling may be done out of love, but it has a detrimental impact. Most families have rules and structures in place that facilitate a safe and cooperative home. These rules and regulations shift from household to household. When there is a child with OCD in a family, the rules and household guidelines need to be shaped to accommodate this unique personality type. At times, enforcing rules on a child with the disorder will cause discomfort, but it is crucial to both their well-being and the mental health of the family.

To maintain healthy familial bonds that mitigate resentment, you need to understand the complexities of OCD and how it can spill over into numerous tasks. Leaving the home can become a strenuous activity if a child with OCD gets trapped in repetitive rituals. Furthermore, it could affect societal perceptions as public outings can trigger strong compulsions. These misunderstandings in social spaces create an alienating aura around an entire family. Therefore, it can delve the familial unit into a cycle of blame, aggression, conflict, and shame. The combination of these negative experiences can create tension that alienates an OCD sufferer within their own homes. Breaking the united front of the family against OCD allows the disorder to contribute toward a litany of other issues that can be extremely destabilizing and unhealthy.

Recognizing the power that OCD has is the first step to making the necessary changes to prevent the disorder from spiraling. You must gather the information to set firm, disorder-appropriate boundaries that acknowledge the collective functioning of a family unit. It is easy to become consumed by the demanding needs of a child with OCD, but you need to take care of yourself, your partner, and any other children you have as well. The needs of the family should not become secondary to the desires of a child with OCD; however, their unique needs must also be incorporated into the system of the family.

Establishing routines and protocols to accommodate everyone in the household, including children with OCD, takes time and concerted effort. Since the disorder is so individualized, the broad practices and philosophies need to be tweaked to work within your personal, familial context. A clear distinction must be made between the child with OCD and the disorder itself. The illness tends to hold homes hostage, but an escape can be crafted with commitment and information. The planning and the work you do to maintain and encourage strong family connections is what will be the key to getting you out of the prison OCD often creates. The effort must come from all participants of a household to be effective so open communication about the realities of the discomfort OCD causes for everybody involved encourages everyone to get on board.

Ripple Effects

Obsessive-compulsive disorder shapes family bonds. The illness will impact parental and sibling relationships. Brothers and sisters of people with OCD report that the disorder bred resentment. One of the major complaints that siblings have is that the disorder can ruin family activities. Due to OCD being thought-triggered, outings to unfamiliar environments can induce compulsions that may throw the entire day off. Maintaining strong relationships between siblings can be difficult when someone has OCD. A sibling may feel like their lives are persistently dictated by the individual with the disorder. This is true to some extent because of the special considerations the sibling needs to consider. Therefore, it is essential to create an open dialogue in group sessions, possibly with a counselor, to address the grievances that siblings have.

Sibling relationships with parents could also be impacted. A brother or a sister may feel like their parents' attention is constantly focused on the child with the disorder. This unequally divided attention may cause them to feel neglected, which could significantly alter their mental and emotional well-being. This neglect is further emphasized by the need to mold their routine around that of their sibling with OCD. Compulsions can often be driven by the mood an individual is in. Anxiety can develop because a sibling cannot gauge how to interact with the child with OCD. Having to walk on eggshells can be taxing for a sibling who is also experiencing their own pressures in life.

In addition to the strain that OCD places on the relationships of siblings, the parental bond will also be affected. Most parents want what is best for their children. The desire to ensure the greatest outcomes for children could drive parents to reshape their whole lives around a child with OCD. This accommodation is unavoidable in some ways, but the persistent effort could cause burnout in a hostage-like environment. Any frameworks that a parent institutes to support their children with OCD should also consider their needs and desires. It is impossible to fill someone with an empty cup, so investing in your own well-being by implementing boundaries and considering your needs will help you be in the right mindset to take care of your children.

Creating a healthy family environment and strengthening bonds with OCD as a factor in your life means that you will have to put in a lot of energy to achieve your vision of a cohesive familial unit. Conflicts will be common, so your resolution toolkit needs to be fully stocked. Informed communication must become a culture in your home because leaving grievances unsaid will only fuel negative feelings. Everyone in the family must be brought on board to build a household that reflects the desires of all the people in the home. The OCD must then be managed according to what most closely aligns with your family's vision. It will be a hard road to travel, but taking your time to communicate and bring together a strong team that tackles the difficulties of OCD while acknowledging the needs of those who do not have the disorder will yield positive outcomes.

Managing Daily Life

Being mindful of the moods of a child who has OCD is an important factor in managing daily life. There will be good days, and there will be terrible days. As difficult as it can be, you must be able to weather the stormier days and accept that these days are a part of the process. When people with OCD feel stressed or emotionally stimulated, their compulsions can become worse. Family-oriented cognitive behavioral therapy, or CBT, can help your child manage their emotions, with the entire household being included to work as a team. CBT allows you to explore your thoughts and feelings in depth to understand how they impact your perceptions and behavior. Having the introspective guide of CBT available to manage emotions can reduce the detrimental impacts of OCD.

Family therapy will help a lot in managing daily tasks. Mental health professionals are better equipped to give you the tasks, activities, and protocols that will alleviate compulsive behavior and create a smoother routine. Considering that everyone in the household will be affected by OCD and will all have grievances related to the disorder, counseling can help unpack and address these issues. The family can then work together on the activities that the therapist suggested and hold one another accountable for behavior that is not aligned with the familial visions and therapeutic agreements.

OCD should not be allowed to hold your child back from forming friendships and participating in extracurricular activities. Although you want to always be present to protect your child with OCD, you must allow some space and freedom so that they can self-actualize. You should focus on giving your child the tools to address their compulsions and trust them enough to implement the techniques. By working with your child and monitoring their progress, you can get them to a position where they can have a life outside of your constant supervision and become a capable and independent individual. Teaching your child effective communication techniques to make their desires known, ask for help when needed, and establish their boundaries will equip them to make friends and engage with their peers at school independently. Your child's OCD may cause you and your family to be overprotective, but you must resist that urge for their social development.

Remember that OCD is a volatile journey. Therefore, you should not make day-to-day comparisons with your child. Avoid saying things like "Last week you did better" or "Before you had OCD, you were able to do this." Instead, focus on celebrating the small victories and reminding your child that their progress is a long-term project. Furthermore, learn to recognize the warning signs of compulsions developing, like changes in their diet or sleeping patterns, as well as spending a longer time doing simple activities or remaining in isolation for extended periods. These signs can help you address compulsions before they grow and get out of hand.

The Martins - A Family's Disruption and Unity

The Martins family has five members: The father, Joseph; the mother, Cassandra; their daughter, Anne, who is sixteen; Kyle, who is twelve; and the youngest, Jonathon, who is eleven and has been diagnosed with OCD for about three years. Jonathon's compulsions cause him to repeatedly open and close doors, as well as knock on hard surfaces. He also repeatedly takes his shoes on and off until he feels comfortable.

Since Johnathon is the youngest, his family wanted to be understanding, so they participated in his compulsions at first and allowed him to go through with his rituals. Eventually, Johnathon's compulsions became disruptive because when he was getting dressed or repeatedly opening and closing doors, it caused the family to be late for engagements. Jonathan's knocking on hard surfaces also caused the family some embarrassment because it could get out of hand in unfamiliar or public places, which resulted in them avoiding going out or visiting other people's homes.

Resentment grew in Kyle and Anne because the family stayed at home most of the time, and they wanted to go out on family outings like they used to before Jonathon was diagnosed. The siblings brought up their complaints with their parents, who often ignored them using the excuse of Jonathon being the youngest and him having OCD. As this persisted, the parents noticed that Kyle and Anne had become emotionally closed off. Furthermore, they had turned cold towards Jonathon by constantly teaming up against him and excluding him from communal activities. The parents' arguments with each other also increased due to the stress that the OCD put on their relationships. The hostile home environment made Jonathon's compulsions worse, so the family had no choice but to address the mounting issues.

The family worked together on drawing up a schedule and setting boundaries on how long

Johnathon could spend knocking on hard surfaces and repeatedly opening and closing doors. It was difficult at first because they constantly had to interrupt Jonathon's compulsions, which brought him great distress. By reassuring Jonathon that everything would be alright even though he was unable to complete his rituals, the family was able to manage and contain his compulsions. The family also decided to do collective cognitive behavioral therapy to manage their emotions and communicate better.

This new routine allowed the family to visit more people and go on more outings while not neglecting Jonathon's unique needs. By working as a cohesive unit, the family was able to create frameworks informed by professional opinions that worked best for them. Everything does not always go smoothly, but they are in a better position than they once were because of communication, cooperation, education, and compromise.

Chapter Takeaways

- OCD is not an individual disorder because it affects all the people around the child suffering from it.

- Communication is key to creating a cohesive family unit where everybody's needs are effectively met.

- The OCD and the child are separate entities, so the family should work together to combat the OCD without alienating the child.

- You cannot allow yourself to be held hostage by OCD, so you must establish boundaries and place limits on how much you indulge in compulsions.

- The aim is to teach your child techniques that can help them manage their OCD so they can become capable and independent.

- Do not sideline your desires and the needs of any other family members who do not have OCD because everybody's feelings are valid.

- Working as a team will help you create a fulfilling daily routine.

OCD does not only affect those who have the disorder, but it has the power to disrupt the lives of the people around the OCD sufferer as well. Therefore, the following chapter dives deep into how you can come together and craft a collective plan to strategically address the disorder. There is strength in unity to overcome adversity.

Chapter 4: Strength in Unity

"Individually, we are one drop. Together, we are an ocean." – Ryunosuke Satoro

OCD can cause isolation in children due to many not understanding the condition. Therefore, as a parent, you can create a community of support that breaks your child free from the ostracizing trap that OCD can become. It can be challenging to offer help in an unfamiliar scenario. However, with the right information and practical tips, you can build networks that maximize the well-being of children with OCD.

With the right tools and support, OCD does not have to be the invisible demon gnawing at your child's ability to have a fulfilling existence. OCD can be morphed into a manageable disorder you do not have to fear. There will inevitably be difficulties when dealing with the often-debilitating condition; however, by establishing a strong support system, you can play a pivotal role in helping your child overcome the hurdles OCD presents.

Rallying against the Unseen Adversary

Unlike more physical ailments, the world cannot see OCD. The disorder is an invisible enemy that prevents progress while the world looks on as if nothing is wrong. Since wider society does not offer much help because of the discreet nature of the illness, it is up to you to construct a team that can rally against this unseen adversary. Figures that play a central role in your child's life will need to be informed and equipped with the skill sets that uplift your child when they have unfounded compulsions. Friends, family, educators, and medical professionals form the team that will assist children experiencing OCD to get the most out of their lives.

Teaching communication is essential to helping your child make use of their support system. Although there are overlaps between the rituals that people with OCD have, the disorder is individualized, with each person having unique expressions of the illness. Therefore, encouraging your child to describe their perceptions and openly talk about their compulsions would create an aura of acceptance, allowing them to understand that they are accepted regardless of their differences.

One way to facilitate openness toward communication is by asking questions and encouraging others who form your child's support system to ask questions as well. When compulsions arise, talk to your child about what is happening. Ask them how they are feeling and what is going through their mind non-judgmentally. This shows that you are attempting to understand their minds and that you have empathy for what they are going through. The instinct of many people is to try to stop the compulsive behavior as soon as it occurs. This approach can cause unnecessary conflict and be alienating. Exercise patience and reassurance so that children with OCD feel safe enough to open up to you about their struggles. Through communication, you will be more informed about what your child is going through and in a better position to offer help.

Do not invalidate the OCD compulsions. This shows that you are not taking your child seriously. Instead, work with them in a controlled setting using ERP or exposure and response prevention. ERP puts the child in an environment that usually induces compulsive behavior, but instead of acting on the compulsions, they do not engage in them. Encouraging a child to resist their compulsions is best done in a low-pressure environment with patient assistance. Community can be used to make this method of treatment more impactful because different people that your child trusts can work with them in a variety of settings. This communal effort will show your child that they are not alone in the battles they face, but they have an army willing to combat adversity with them.

Society may not understand what OCD is due to media misinformation and simply not having encountered the illness before. However, you can create a community that is informed and driven to assist your child. This turns the invisible disorder into a monster that is collectively tackled. Structuring a supportive group of people who understand the intricacies of OCD could be life-altering when it comes to benefiting your child and encouraging them to reach their full potential.

Your team of friends, family, educators, and medical professionals will be the podium your child stands on to claim their victories. Moreover, your network will be the shoulder they cry on when they have losses. You are sowing together a comforting quilt of knowledge, emotional support, and practical advice that gives your child the best possible shot at overcoming the hurdles of OCD to achieve the highest levels of personal fulfillment.

Externalizing OCD

OCD is not who your child is; it is only a part of their identity. Compulsive behaviors might seem like they are taking over your child's life; however, this does not need to become their identity. The illness will shape parts of who they are, but it doesn't need to become central to how they define themselves. To help your child understand OCD as being separate from who they are, you can use certain techniques to help externalize the disorder. Furthermore, externalizing OCD will help the people around your child identify what is happening and when they may need assistance. Communicating about OCD becomes a lot easier when the illness is externalized.

One of the easiest ways to externalize OCD is by giving it a name. Naming one's OCD helps demystify the disorder and can help in speaking about the illness openly and accurately. Take the name "Michelle," for example. When a child has compulsions or is feeling stressed out enough that impulsive behaviors start to occur, they can say something like, "I think Michelle is about to show up." A parent can then ask, "What does Michelle want to do?" or "Why is Michelle making an appearance?" Naming OCD makes it less intimidating and integrates it as a part of your child's life instead of framing it as an all-consuming dragon you can do nothing about.

Furthermore, externalizing OCD can turn it into a challenge you are tackling with your child instead of having them feel like it is a battle they are fighting alone. By separating the OCD as a core part of your child's personality, the actions you take to help alleviate compulsions will not feel like an attack on your child but rather like collectively combating the disorder. Any uncomfortable actions that a child with OCD takes will not feel like their parent is trying to hurt them because they understand that their OCD is, in essence, not them. Externalizing OCD profoundly reinforces the idea that the child is not their disorder.

The language you use when discussing your child's OCD will also contribute to how the disorder is internalized. Instead of "your" compulsions or "your" obsessive behaviors, use words like "a" compulsion or "the" obsessive behaviors. When you put "your" in front of words that relate to the disorder, it can come off as blaming or demeaning. You can even restructure sentences to avoid putting ownership onto compulsive behaviors, like "She is experiencing a compulsion" instead of "She has compulsions." The difference between these two sentences may seem minor; however, using "she has" and not "she is experiencing" tends to feel like internalizing language. The aim is to separate the disorder from a child's identity, so any language that takes ownership of the illness should be discouraged. It is not that you are in denial about the illness, but rather using externalizing language when discussing OCD to emphasize that their compulsions are not a part of them and just something they are going through. By avoiding taking hold of the disorder as their own, a child is better equipped to make decisions that relieve the symptoms of OCD.

Considering that compulsive behaviors do not spring up out of nowhere and are stimulated by certain triggers, externalizing one's experience with compulsions will help identify triggering environments better. A child who thinks they just have compulsive behaviors sometimes, rather than realizing that their compulsions are brought about by stressful situations, is ill-equipped to make decisions that increase their well-being. Externalizing OCD is like grabbing the illness in your hand and moving it around to examine it from all angles.

The societal stigma around OCD will always exist because of ignorance and the lack of interaction with the disorder. This alienation may cause your child to feel like they are inadequate. Therefore, you are in a constant battle of reminding your child that OCD does not make them any less of a person than anybody else. Externalizing the disorder as a defining factor of the core of them as an individual opens the pathway to seeing themselves as more than an afflicted child. Your child's self-perception does not need to be encapsulated in their experiences with OCD because they can progress with your help by framing the illness as an obstacle instead of a crutch.

Refocusing Attention

Refocusing one's attention can alleviate compulsions. OCD forces the mind to focus on repetitive tasks because the person experiencing the disorder feels discomfort if they do not complete compulsive rituals. Therefore, redirecting the mind helps them address the compulsions induced by OCD. For example, your child can begin listing all the items they see in a room, or they can say the alphabet backward. These kinds of focus-related games are a great tool to use in difficult times when they feel trapped by their compulsions. Learning these distraction techniques can be a blessing for creating a resilient attitude. Stress and anxiety are triggers for OCD rituals. Thus, mindfulness is a useful technique to escape compulsions. Mindfulness is all about slowing down and bringing yourself into the current moment. Through mindful breathing, meditation, and yoga, your child can be taught to non-judgmentally analyze their thoughts and feelings, which could help them work through the kinds of stress that cause their OCD compulsions to activate.

You will not always be around to guide your child and be a support structure, so their resilience needs to develop independently of you. Encourage your child to communicate openly with the people around them, like friends or peers, so that they can get an understanding of the behaviors that seem foreign to them. This way, when you are not around, the people your child is with can be the assistance your child needs in your absence. Open communication coupled with the practices of mindfulness, ERP, and refocusing the mind gives your child the ingredients needed to develop resilience.

Journaling also works wonders when creating an impenetrable and durable mindset for children with OCD. Writing down your thoughts and emotions is a gateway to understanding yourself and your mind better.

Buy your child a journal and encourage them to write in it every day. Prompt them to write about how their day went, how they felt, and how their compulsions affected them. This allows your child to explore themselves in detail, free from any external forces. The independence that journaling will introspectively build is central to cultivating resilience.

The Role of Therapy

As much as your heart is in the right place, a qualified professional is better equipped to assist your child in certain ways than you are. Allowing a professional without any direct links to your child to take the lead in certain instances can be extremely difficult. However, there are major benefits to seeking out therapy to help with OCD.

Therapy and counseling help your child understand their thoughts and emotions better. This understanding will help them navigate their compulsions so that they are no longer as sensitive to them. Therapists have studied human psychology in excruciating detail. This allows therapists to respond to the needs of your child from an informed place. They can pick up subtle details and indicators that it is easy for an untrained eye to miss. Therefore, consulting a therapist may be the best option for helping your child address the stagnating impacts of their OCD.

Thoughts and emotions are the driving forces behind the compulsion's indicative of OCD. With cognitive behavioral therapy, your child will be taught how to deeply engage with their thoughts, the origins of what they are thinking, and why they are processing information in the way that they do. This puts your child in a position of power instead of falling victim to the processes of their mind. By putting themselves into the driver's seat, your child can respond to the obstructions in the road that OCD presents.

Chapter Takeaways

- Obsessive-compulsive disorder can be an isolating illness; therefore, you need to support your child along the journey.

- Creating an environment where open and honest communication can take place is beneficial for building a relationship where your child is willing to share their concerns and challenges.

- Encourage your child to communicate with their peers and other people around them so that their behavior can be better understood.

- Coping activities like refocusing their mind, mindfulness meditation, journaling, and ERP can help your child build the resilience needed to thrive with OCD.

- Allow your child to explore themselves non-judgmentally to independently find ways to deal with their OCD that work for them.

- Emphasize that having OCD is only a part of your child's personality and not their identity.

- Never invalidate your child's experiences with obsessive rituals, and patiently practice with them to develop the tools needed to address the symptoms of OCD.

- Give compulsive behaviors induced by OCD a name like "Michelle," so your child can understand that these rituals are not who they are and so that you can better help your child address these issues without them feeling like you are attacking them.

- Work with your social group and networks by honestly communicating so that they can assist you in creating an environment conducive to the growth and well-being of your child.

The next chapter will delve into the details of Exposure Response Prevention, or ERP, which is one of the leading interventions for treating OCD. Understanding how ERP works and why it can be detrimental to enabling your child's OCD impulses is fundamental to crafting a winning strategy against the disorder. The chapter will outline how ERP is applied and how parents can assist their children to ensure success with using the method.

Chapter 5: Guiding Light

"Do the thing you fear the most, and it will be the certain death of it." — Ralph Waldo Emerson.

What Is ERP?

Exposure Response Prevention (ERP) is a specialized form of cognitive-behavioral therapy (CBT) primarily used to treat OCD. It's rooted in the understanding that OCD is characterized by distressing obsessions (repetitive, intrusive, and unwanted thoughts) and compulsions (repetitive behaviors or mental acts performed in response to obsessions to alleviate anxiety). ERP aims to break the cycle of OCD by systematically confronting and reducing these obsessions and compulsions.

Key Components of ERP

Exposure

ERP's "exposure" component involves deliberately exposing individuals to situations, thoughts, or triggers that provoke their obsessions. These exposures are carefully planned and tailored to the individual's specific obsessions.

Response Prevention

The "response prevention" aspect is about preventing individuals from engaging in the typical compulsive behaviors or rituals that they use to reduce the distress or anxiety caused by their obsessions. They will be encouraged to resist the urge to perform these compulsions.

Why ERP Is Effective

Targets the Root Cause

ERP directly addresses the underlying mechanisms of OCD rather than merely managing the symptoms. It acknowledges that the obsessions drive the compulsions and prioritizes dissecting these obsessions.

Brain Rewiring

ERP rewires the brain's response to obsessions. Repeating exposing individuals to their fears and preventing their compulsive responses teaches the brain that the feared consequences don't occur. This leads to habituation, where the anxiety naturally decreases over time.

Gradual Exposure

ERP employs a systematic approach, beginning with less distressing triggers and progressing to more challenging ones. This gradual exposure helps individuals build confidence and tolerance.

Empowerment

ERP empowers individuals to confront their fears and obsessions in a controlled and supportive environment. It allows them to regain a sense of control over their lives, which can be transformative.

Reduced Reliance on Compulsions

Through ERP, individuals learn that they can tolerate their anxiety without resorting to compulsions. This, in turn, reduces their reliance on rituals and leads to long-term symptom reduction.

Evidence-Based

ERP is supported by extensive scientific research. Numerous studies have consistently shown its effectiveness in treating OCD across different age groups, including children and adults.

Customized Treatment

ERP is highly individualized. Therapists work closely with individuals to tailor exposure exercises to their specific obsessions and compulsions, ensuring a personalized treatment plan.

Long-Term Benefits

ERP offers not just short-term relief but also long-term benefits. Many individuals who complete ERP experience significant reductions in OCD symptoms and improvements in their overall quality of life.

Versatility

While ERP is primarily associated with OCD treatment, its exposure and response prevention principles are versatile and can be adapted for other anxiety disorders and phobias.

Therapist Support

ERP is conducted by a trained therapist who provides support, guidance, and feedback throughout the treatment process.

ERP is a robust and evidence-based therapy for OCD that directly targets the core features of the disorder. Exposing individuals to their obsessions while preventing compulsive responses helps change their brain's response to anxiety, ultimately leading to significant and long-lasting symptom reduction. Its customizability, therapist support, and proven track record make it a highly effective treatment for OCD and related anxiety disorders.

The Power of Exposure Response Prevention (ERP)

Assessment and Planning

Before starting ERP, a thorough assessment of the child's OCD symptoms is made by a trained therapist. This assessment helps identify specific obsessions, compulsions, triggers, and the severity of the disorder.

Based on the assessment, a customized ERP treatment plan is developed. The plan outlines the hierarchy of exposure situations, starting with less distressing triggers and progressing to more challenging ones.

Psychoeducation

The child and their family are educated about OCD, its nature, and how ERP works. Understanding that OCD is a brain-based disorder can reduce stigma and help the child and family approach treatment with empathy and patience.

Building a Fear Hierarchy

The therapist and child work together to create a fear hierarchy. This is a list of situations or triggers that cause anxiety and distress, ranked from least to most distressing.

For example, if a child has contamination obsessions, the hierarchy might include touching a "contaminated" object, touching a doorknob, and eventually touching something perceived as very dirty.

Exposure Exercises

Exposure exercises are designed to systematically confront the child with items or situations from their fear hierarchy. These exercises should be completed with the therapist to ensure safety and effectiveness.

The child is exposed to the anxiety-provoking situation without engaging in any compulsive behaviors. They are encouraged to sit with the discomfort and anxiety that arises.

Response Prevention

The "response prevention" aspect of ERP is crucial. It involves preventing the child from performing their go-to compulsions or rituals to alleviate their anxiety.

For example, if a child's compulsion is washing their hands excessively due to contamination fears, they are asked to refrain from washing their hands after touching a feared object.

Gradual Exposure

ERP follows a gradual exposure approach, starting with less distressing situations and progressively moving towards more challenging ones as the child gains confidence.

The therapist and child work together to ensure the exposures are manageable but still anxiety-provoking.

Anxiety Tolerance

Children are taught skills to tolerate the anxiety that arises during exposure exercises. They learn that anxiety naturally decreases over time without engaging in compulsions.

Repetition and Homework

ERP is not a one-time fix; it requires repetition and practice. Children are encouraged to repeat exposure exercises regularly in therapy sessions and as homework assignments.

Homework assignments help generalize the skills learned in therapy to real-life situations, reinforcing the child's ability to resist compulsions.

Therapist Support

The therapist provides guidance, support, and feedback throughout the ERP process. They help the child and their family navigate challenges and make necessary adjustments to the treatment plan.

Progress Tracking

Progress is monitored and tracked regularly. The child and therapist assess changes in OCD symptoms and adjust the treatment plan accordingly.

ERP is a powerful and evidence-based therapy for OCD because it directly addresses the core mechanisms of the disorder. By systematically exposing the child to their fears and preventing compulsive responses, ERP helps them adjust their brain's response to obsessions, reducing the intensity and frequency of OCD symptoms. It empowers children to regain control over their lives and reduce the impact of OCD on their daily functioning and overall well-being.

The power of ERP lies in its ability to break the cycle of OCD. By exposing the child to their fears and preventing the compulsive response, ERP helps them learn that their anxieties are manageable and that they don't need to rely on rituals to feel better. Over time, this reduces the grip OCD has on the child's life and leads to significant symptom reduction.

Parents need to actively support their child during ERP treatment, as it can be challenging. Still, the long-term benefits of reduced OCD symptoms and improved quality of life make it an efficient approach to helping children break free from OCD's clutches. Always consult a mental health professional for a proper assessment and guidance on implementing ERP for your child.

Parental Role in ERP

The role of parents in Exposure Response Prevention (ERP) therapy for a child with Obsessive-Compulsive Disorder (OCD) is crucial. Parents need to be a source of support and encouragement during the treatment process. Of course, it's essential to strike a balance, which you can do with the tips below.

Education and Understanding

Parents should take the time to educate themselves about OCD. Understanding the nature of the disorder, its symptoms, and how ERP therapy works will make you feel more confident in assisting your child through their journey. This knowledge helps parents approach the treatment process with empathy and informed support.

Active Participation

Be actively involved in your child's treatment. Collaborate closely with the therapist and attend therapy sessions when appropriate to gain insights into your child's progress and therapy goals.

Create a Supportive Environment

Foster a safe and understanding home environment where your child feels comfortable discussing their OCD-related fears and challenges. Encourage open communication without judgment.

Encourage Compliance

Support your child in attending therapy sessions regularly and completing homework assignments as prescribed by the therapist. Consistency is vital for the success of ERP.

Avoid Accommodating OCD

One of the most critical aspects of supporting ERP is not accommodating or enabling OCD behaviors. This means not participating in or assisting with compulsions or rituals.

Avoid providing reassurance or making special accommodations to reduce your child's distress, as this can reinforce OCD patterns.

Patience and Empathy

ERP can be challenging for your child, and they will experience anxiety during exposure exercises. Work on being patient, empathetic, and supportive while also not giving in to compulsions.

Model Calm and Tolerance

Demonstrate calm and tolerance when your child experiences anxiety or distress related to their OCD. Your behavior can serve as a model for how to manage anxiety effectively.

Set Realistic Expectations

Understand that progress in ERP is gradual. Set realistic expectations for improvement and acknowledge and celebrate small victories along the way.

Avoid Criticism or Blame

Refrain from blaming or criticizing your child for their OCD symptoms. OCD is not a choice, and negative comments can increase their anxiety and guilt.

Encourage Independence

As your child gains confidence in managing their OCD, encourage them to take more responsibility for their treatment. This will help them build self-efficacy and a sense of control.

Seek Support for Yourself

Caring for a child with OCD can be emotionally challenging. Consider seeking support for yourself, such as through therapy or support groups, to help you manage your own stress and emotions between being supportive and not enabling OCD behaviors.

Be Flexible and Adaptive

Be willing to adjust your approach as your child progresses in therapy. As they become more capable of managing their OCD, the level of support and intervention you provide may need to change.

Maintain Boundaries

Set clear boundaries with your child about what behaviors are acceptable and what are not. Consistently reinforce these boundaries to avoid enabling OCD.

Celebrate Progress

Celebrate your child's progress and achievements in ERP. Positive reinforcement can motivate them to continue working on their treatment.

Remember that ERP can be challenging for both you and your child, but it is one of the most effective treatments for OCD. By providing support while avoiding enabling behaviors, you can play a vital role in helping your child break free from the trap of OCD and lead a healthier, more fulfilling life. Always consult with your child's therapist for specific guidance on how to best support your child's ERP treatment.

Success Stories

Here are a few success stories of children who have benefited from ERP:

Sarah's Freedom from Contamination Fears

Background: Sarah, a 10-year-old girl, developed severe contamination fears that began to disrupt her daily life. She believed touching "dirty" objects would harm her, so she compulsively washed her hands to avoid this perceived danger.

ERP Therapy: Sarah's therapist began ERP therapy by creating a hierarchy of exposure tasks. Initially, they touched harmless but "dirty" objects like a doorknob and gradually progressed to more anxiety-inducing items. Sarah was encouraged to resist handwashing after each exposure, experiencing the discomfort of her anxiety.

Progress: Over several weeks, Sarah's fear decreased as she faced her contamination fears head-on. She learned to tolerate the discomfort without washing her hands excessively. By the end of therapy, Sarah attended school regularly, played with friends, and engaged in activities without the constant need to wash her hands.

Tom's Escape from Checking Compulsions

Background: Tom, a 13-year-old boy, suffered from debilitating checking compulsions. He believed that his family's safety depended on his repeatedly checking locks, appliances, and switches, making it challenging for him to leave home.

ERP Therapy: Tom's therapist designed a structured ERP program, starting with less anxiety-provoking scenarios. Tom was gradually exposed to the idea of not acting on his checking compulsions as frequently. His therapist helped him grow to resist these compulsions.

After thorough evaluation and assessment, Tom's therapist identified specific triggers, obsessions, and compulsions associated with Tom's checking behavior. The triggers were conveyed to Tom and his family, letting them understand the nature of OCD, the cycle of obsessions, and the rationale behind ERP therapy. The next step involved devising a hierarchy of triggers related to Tom's checking compulsions, which included situations or objects that trigger anxiety and lead to checking behaviors. The therapist developed a series of exposure exercises based on the hierarchy with Tom on board. These exercises made Tom face anxiety-provoking situations while limiting his compulsive checking behavior. For example, suppose Tom gets anxious about the window being open. In that case, an exposure exercise where the window is intentionally left open will be introduced. Tom must experience a thought-provoking situation during this routine until the anxiety decreases. This type of exposure exercise is known as habituation.

With his family's aid, Tom started these exposure exercises and gradually progressed from the least distressing exposure exercises to more challenging ones as he developed confidence in managing his anxiety. Tom's therapist also provided home assignments and maintenance strategies to maintain his progress. Parents and the therapist provided ongoing support and monitoring to ensure the ERP program was followed and addressed any challenges or setbacks Tom encountered during the program.

Progress: Through ERP therapy, Tom gained confidence in managing his anxiety without excessive checking. He practiced these skills daily and was eventually able to leave home for school without extensive checking rituals. His family noticed an improvement in his daily functioning, and he regained his independence.

Emily's Victory over Intrusive Thoughts

Background: 16-year-old Emily struggled with distressing; intrusive thoughts related to harm coming to her loved ones. These thoughts caused intense anxiety and guilt, driving her to engage in lengthy mental rituals to neutralize them.

ERP Therapy: Emily's therapist used ERP to expose her to anxiety-provoking situations. Emily was encouraged to deliberately bring up her intrusive thoughts and resist the compulsion to perform mental rituals like counting or repeating phrases to neutralize the anxiety.

Progress: Throughout therapy, Emily learned to tolerate the discomfort of her intrusive thoughts. With her therapist's guidance, she developed strategies to reframe her thinking and manage her anxiety. Emily was eventually able to focus on her schoolwork and social life without the constant burden of intrusive thoughts, greatly improving her quality of life.

Ben's Triumph over Hoarding Behaviors

Background: When 14-year-old Ben started struggling with hoarding behaviors, they quickly took over his bedroom. His room was cluttered to the point where he couldn't use it for its intended purpose, and it caused distress.

ERP Therapy: Ben's therapist worked closely with him and his family to create a plan to address the hoarding behaviors. They started by sorting through items in his room, deciding what to keep, discard, or donate. Ben was gradually exposed to discarding items and resisting the urge to hoard with ongoing support from his therapist and family.

Progress: Ben transformed his room into a functional space over several months. He learned valuable skills for organization and decision-making, which helped prevent relapse. With his newfound living space and the ability to maintain it, Ben's overall well-being and family relationships improved significantly.

Sophia's Triumph over Symmetry Obsessions

Background: Sophia was only 9 years old when she developed an obsession with symmetry. She believed that something terrible would happen to her family if things weren't perfectly balanced. This obsession led her to spend hours rearranging objects in her home.

ERP Therapy: Sophia's therapist recognized her symmetry obsession and created a gradual exposure plan. They started with minor asymmetrical arrangements and worked their way up to more significant challenges. Throughout therapy, Sophia was encouraged to resist the compulsion to rearrange.

Progress: Sophia's fear of asymmetry eventually diminished as she confronted it directly. She gained confidence in her ability to tolerate the discomfort and was gradually able to let go of her compulsive behaviors. She ended up spending more time on her interests, such as art and playing with friends, without being consumed by symmetrical concerns.

Jacob's Journey to Overcome Aggressive Thoughts

Background: At 15, Jacob experienced distressing, aggressive thoughts about harming others, even though he had no intention of acting on them. These thoughts caused him great anxiety and guilt, and he often avoided social interactions to prevent potential harm.

ERP Therapy: Jacob was guided by a therapist with the use of ERP to confront these thoughts and resist the urge to avoid social situations. This helped him develop cognitive strategies to reframe these thoughts as meaningless and disconnected from his true intentions.

Progress: With consistent therapy, Jacob learned to tolerate the discomfort of his intrusive thoughts without resorting to avoidance or compulsive behaviors. He gradually re-engaged in social activities and better understood his thought patterns. Although the thoughts didn't disappear entirely, Jacob was able to manage them and lead a more fulfilling and socially active life.

These additional stories illustrate the versatility of ERP therapy in treating various OCD symptoms in children and adolescents. ERP can be customized to address each individual's unique obsessions and compulsions, ultimately helping them regain control over their lives and reduce the interference of OCD in their daily functioning.

Chapter Takeaways

Exposure Response Prevention (ERP)

- ERP is an evidence-based therapy for Obsessive-Compulsive Disorder (OCD).
- It involves exposing individuals to their fears (exposure) and preventing them from

engaging in compulsive behaviors (response prevention).

- ERP directly addresses the root causes of OCD and rewires the brain's response to obsessions.
- Gradual exposure, empowerment, and long-term benefits are some of its key features.

Parental Role in ERP

- Parents play a vital role in supporting their child's ERP therapy for OCD.
- They should educate themselves about OCD and actively participate in the treatment process.
- Creating a supportive environment, encouraging therapy compliance, and avoiding the accommodation of OCD behaviors are essential.
- Parents should be patient, empathetic, and model calmness and tolerance.
- Although the path to empower your child and face their fears will be difficult, a collective family effort and persistent support can surely result in progress.

Success Stories of Children Benefiting from ERP

- ERP therapy has helped numerous children overcome OCD.
- Success stories highlight children's triumphs over various OCD symptoms, such as handwashing, checking rituals, intrusive thoughts, and avoidance behaviors.
- The therapy's effectiveness is credited to gradual exposure, support from therapists, and parental involvement.
- These takeaways provide a comprehensive understanding of ERP therapy, the parental role in supporting children with OCD, and real-life success stories demonstrating the therapy's positive impact on young individuals.

The next chapter uncovers the connection between the brain and gut and how this connection is related to OCD.

Chapter 6: The Mind-Gut Connection

"Don't let OCD control your life. You are in charge, not the disorder." – Charlize Theron

Since birth, humans develop a bi-directional communication system between the gastrointestinal tract (GI tract) and the brain, referred to in medical terminology as the gut-brain axis. This communication channel arises out of complex interactions between the central nervous system (CNS) controlling the brain and three other systems, namely the immune system (the body's defense system against diseases), the endocrine system (hormone-producing system), and the enteric nervous system (ENS), which controls gut functions. Any medical condition, environmental triggers, or factors that affect the brain or the alimentary system can produce a ripple effect, disrupting several metabolic processes linked to mental well-being and physical health.

This disruption can potentially increase the risk of developing anxiety disorders or trigger certain mental illnesses that may contribute to developing OCD in children.

The Role of Gut Microbiota

Whether it's a child or an adult, the alimentary system is home to trillions of gut-friendly microorganisms that aid digestion and improve overall health. When a disease, certain foods, or any external factor kills this gut microbiota, it affects the gut-brain axis, subsequently influencing children's mood, cognition, and behavior. These negative influences on the child can potentially trigger the development of anxiety disorders like OCD.

Besides gut microbiota changes, any other influential factor disrupting the gut-brain axis in children will negatively affect physical and mental health and significantly increase the risk of developing neurological disorders. Scientists and researchers have already developed novel therapeutic approaches like probiotics, prebiotics, and dietary changes and have devised several interventions to indirectly improve mental health.

The gut-brain connection is a complex and dynamic communication network involving neurons, hormones, signaling molecules, gut microbiota, immune system, and stress response. It is fundamental in regulating physiological processes and influencing mood, behavior, and overall well-being. Ongoing research unveils this connection's intricate mechanisms and therapeutic potential for physical and mental health.

Nourishing Brain Health

Nourishing brain health in children with Obsessive-Compulsive Disorder (OCD) is essential for their overall well-being and can complement traditional therapies like Exposure Response Prevention (ERP) therapy. Here are some strategies and practices to promote brain health in children with OCD:

Balanced Nutrition

Ensure your child maintains a balanced diet rich in essential nutrients, including omega-3 fatty acids, antioxidants, vitamins, and minerals. Omega-3s, found in fish like salmon and walnuts, have been linked to improved brain health.

Hydration

Proper hydration is necessary for brain function. Encourage your child to drink an adequate amount of water throughout the day.

Limit Sugar and Processed Foods

Reduce the intake of sugary and processed foods. These can lead to fluctuations in blood sugar levels, affecting mood and energy levels.

Regular Exercise

Physical activity is not only beneficial for physical health but also for brain health. Regular exercise reduces anxiety and improves overall well-being.

Adequate Sleep

Sleep is essential for memory consolidation, emotional regulation, and overall cognitive function, so make sure your child gets an adequate amount of sleep each night.

Stress Management

Teach your child stress management techniques such as deep breathing exercises, mindfulness, and progressive muscle relaxation. These techniques reduce anxiety, which is associated with OCD.

Cognitive Stimulation

Encourage activities that stimulate cognitive function, such as reading, puzzles, board games, and creative activities like drawing or writing.

Social Connection

Foster a supportive social environment for your child. Positive social interactions have a big impact on emotional well-being and brain health.

Limit Screen Time

Limit screen time and ensure that the content your child engages with is age appropriate. Excessive screen time can impact sleep quality and emotional well-being.

Structured Routine

Establish a structured daily routine. Predictable schedules soothe a child's anxiety and provide stability for those with OCD.

Professional Guidance

Work closely with healthcare professionals and therapists to create a well-rounded treatment plan that meets your child's needs. A professional will guide you on medication, therapy, and lifestyle changes.

Medication as Prescribed

If a healthcare provider prescribes medication, ensure your child takes it as directed. Medication can be a helpful component of OCD treatment when used with therapy.

Family Support

Engage in family therapy or support groups to learn how to support your child best. Educate family members about OCD to create a supportive environment.

Positive Reinforcement

Encourage and reward your child's progress and achievements in managing their OCD. Positive reinforcement motivates them to continue working on their treatment.

Every child with OCD is unique; what works best for one child may not work for another. Consulting with a mental health professional specializing in OCD cases helps you develop a tailored plan to nourish your child's brain health and support their journey toward managing their OCD effectively.

Probiotics and Mental Health

Gut Microbiota and Mental Health

As explained earlier, the gut microbiota consists of trillions of microorganisms in the gastrointestinal tract, including bacteria. Emerging research has revealed the profound influence of the gut microbiota on mental health through the microbiota-gut-brain axis. Disruptions in the balance of gut bacteria (dysbiosis) have been linked to mood disorders such as depression, anxiety, and even neurodegenerative diseases.

Serotonin Production

Serotonin is a neurotransmitter that plays a role in mood regulation. Approximately 90% of serotonin is produced in the gut, specifically in the enterochromaffin cells. These cells are in close communication with the gut microbiota. Probiotics help maintain a balanced gut microbiota, possibly indirectly supporting serotonin synthesis. A healthier gut environment fosters the conditions necessary for optimal serotonin production.

Reduction of Inflammation

Chronic inflammation has been implicated in the development and exacerbation of mood disorders. Dysbiosis in the gut can contribute to inflammation. Probiotics, particularly those with anti-inflammatory properties, help restore gut microbiota balance, reducing systemic inflammation and potentially improving mental health.

Stress Response Modulation

The gut-brain axis also assists in stress response regulation. A balanced gut microbiota enhances resilience to stress by modulating the release of stress hormones like cortisol. Probiotics may influence the gut-brain axis to help mitigate the effects of stress on mental health.

Gut-Brain Communication

The communication between the gut and the brain occurs through various pathways, including the vagus nerve, the immune system, and the production of signaling molecules. Probiotics can influence this communication by producing metabolites and molecules that signal the brain. This may impact mood, cognition, and behavior.

Anxiety and Depression

While more research is needed to establish definitive links, some studies suggest that certain probiotic strains may benefit anxiety and depression symptoms. For example, the Lactobacillus and Bifidobacterium genera have been investigated for their potential to reduce symptoms of anxiety and depression.

Magnesium and Mental Health

Neurotransmitter Regulation

Magnesium regulates neurotransmitters in the brain, including serotonin and dopamine. These neurotransmitters play key roles in mood regulation and overall mental health. Adequate magnesium levels support these neurotransmitters' production, release, and function, positively impacting mood and emotional well-being.

Stress Reduction

Magnesium has a calming effect on the nervous system. It can block certain receptors in the brain responsible for the "fight or flight" stress response. By reducing the reactivity of the stress response system, magnesium can lower anxiety levels and improve overall mental resilience to stress.

Sleep Improvement

Magnesium is essential for regulating melatonin, the hormone controlling sleep-wake cycles. Adequate magnesium levels help maintain a healthy sleep pattern, improving sleep quality and reducing the risk of mood disturbances associated with sleep deprivation.

Migraine Prevention

Magnesium supplementation has shown promise in reducing some individuals' migraines' frequency and severity. Mood disturbances and anxiety often accompany migraines. By preventing or alleviating migraines, magnesium may indirectly benefit mental health by reducing these associated mood disruptions.

Depression Management

Low magnesium levels have been associated with depression, and studies suggest that magnesium supplementation may positively impact depressive symptoms. The mechanisms behind this potential benefit may involve regulating neurotransmitters and reducing inflammation, which are closely linked to depression.

Probiotics and magnesium are two dietary components that greatly influence mental health through various mechanisms. Probiotics support a healthy gut microbiota, impacting neurotransmitter production, inflammation, and stress response regulation. Magnesium is involved in neurotransmitter regulation, stress reduction, sleep improvement, migraine prevention, and depression management. While these nutrients offer potential mental health benefits, consulting with a healthcare professional for personalized guidance is necessary, especially when addressing specific mental health concerns.

Benefits of the Anti-inflammatory Diet

Reduced Chronic Inflammation

Chronic inflammation is a long-term, low-grade immune response that can damage cells and tissues over time. It is linked to numerous chronic diseases, including cardiovascular disease, type 2 diabetes, cancer, and autoimmune disorders. The Anti-Inflammatory Diet focuses on foods that reduce inflammation, such as fruit, vegetables, whole grains, and healthy fats, while limiting or avoiding foods that cause inflammation, including refined sugars, trans fats, and processed meats. By adopting this diet, individuals will reduce their overall inflammatory load, potentially lowering their risk of developing inflammation-related chronic diseases.

Improved Heart Health

Chronic inflammation is a significant risk factor for heart disease. Inflammation can damage blood vessels and contribute to the buildup of arterial plaque. The Anti-Inflammatory Diet promotes heart-healthy foods like fruit, vegetables, nuts, seeds, and fatty fish rich in omega-3 fatty acids. These foods lower inflammation and support heart health. Additionally, the diet recommends minimizing or eliminating processed foods and unhealthy fats that contribute to heart disease.

Better Blood Sugar Control

Chronic inflammation can interfere with insulin sensitivity and contribute to insulin resistance, a key factor in developing type 2 diabetes. The Anti-Inflammatory Diet includes complex carbohydrates from whole grains, fiber-rich foods, and lean proteins. These food choices stabilize blood sugar levels and improve insulin sensitivity. By managing blood sugar effectively, individuals can reduce their risk of developing type 2 diabetes or better control the condition if already diagnosed.

Weight Management

Obesity and chronic inflammation are closely linked. Adipose tissue (fat cells) can produce inflammatory molecules, contributing to systemic inflammation. The Anti-Inflammatory Diet prioritizes whole, nutrient-dense foods that are filling and satisfying. Individuals can manage their calorie intake and support weight management goals by reducing processed foods, added sugars, and unhealthy fats.

Sample Meals on the Anti-inflammatory Diet

Breakfast

- **Overnight oats**: Combine rolled oats, chia seeds, almond milk, and a topping of berries and walnuts. Add a drizzle of honey or maple syrup if desired.

- Scrambled eggs with sautéed spinach, diced tomatoes, and sliced avocado. Serve with whole-grain toast.

Lunch

- **Grilled chicken or tofu salad:** Combine mixed greens, cherry tomatoes, cucumber slices, and bell peppers. Dress with a homemade vinaigrette made from olive oil and lemon juice.

- **Quinoa and black bean bowl:** Prepare quinoa and black beans, roast vegetables like sweet potatoes and broccoli, and drizzle with tahini sauce for added flavor.

Dinner

- **Baked salmon**: Season salmon fillets with herbs and lemon, then bake. Serve with a side of steamed broccoli and cooked quinoa.

- **Lentil and vegetable curry**: Make a flavorful curry with various vegetables and spices. Serve over brown rice.

Snacks

- Greek yogurt with a sprinkle of almonds and fresh fruit like berries or sliced peaches.

- Snack on carrot and celery sticks with hummus for a satisfying and fiber-rich option.

- Enjoy a bowl of mixed berries with a dollop of Greek yogurt for a healthy, anti-inflammatory dessert.

Success Stories on the Anti-inflammatory Diet

Jason's Journey in Managing Childhood OCD with the Anti-Inflammatory Diet

A ten-year-old boy, Jason, had been struggling with OCD for several years. Concerned about OCD's impact on his daily life, his parents sought alternate approaches to compliment Jason's ongoing therapy. After extensive research, they stumbled upon information regarding an anti-inflammatory diet and the numerous benefits that come with its adoption.

Adoption of the Anti-Inflammatory Diet

Jason's parents began understanding the impact of an anti-inflammatory diet on symptoms of OCD in children. The child's therapist and a pediatric dietitian were on board to create a personalized, child-friendly plan. This plan focused on incorporating foods with anti-inflammatory properties into Jason's diet. The pediatric dietician meticulously included fruits, vegetables, lean proteins, healthy fats, and whole grains in the required ratio to provide the desired anti-inflammatory effects and a balanced meal. Inflammatory foods like sugary snacks and processed items were stopped to improve the outcomes of the diet plan.

Results and Progress

Over time, Jason experienced significant improvements in his OCD symptoms and overall well-being. The intensity and frequency of his obsessive thoughts and compulsive behaviors decreased significantly. Although it took some time, Jason finally became capable of managing his symptoms by himself.

Improved Mood: Over time, the pressure Jason felt due to OCD symptoms reduced, which improved his mood. He became happier, relaxed and started engaging in schoolwork and social activities while keeping his obsessive behaviors and thoughts at bay.

Better Sleep: His parents also noticed an improvement in Jason's sleep patterns. He could now sleep more soundly and started following a timetable for bedtime and waking up, improving his sleep quality and overall well-being.

Increased Participation: As the intensity and frequency of OCD symptoms started decreasing, Jason felt motivated and confident when participating in extracurricular activities at school, playing sports, and painting, which he mostly avoided engaging in due to his OCD.

Maintaining the Lifestyle

Encouraged by Jason's progress, the parents incorporated an anti-inflammatory diet as a long-term lifestyle choice. The pediatric dietician also played a significant role in devising and tweaking meals to keep Jason engaged and excited about his diet. Besides adopting an anti-inflammatory diet, therapy sessions and the implementation of stress management techniques were also carried out.

Jason's journey demonstrates how the Anti-Inflammatory Diet, designed in consultation with a pediatric dietitian, can complement therapy for childhood OCD. Incorporating this effective intervention under the guidance of a healthcare professional can significantly improve the well-being of children with OCD.

Emma's Triumph in Managing Childhood OCD

Emma, an eleven-year-old girl, had been struggling with social challenges and issues with obsessive-compulsive disorder (OCD) for a few years. Although Emma was taking the required therapy to manage her OCD, her parents wanted to further improve her quality of life by minimizing the symptoms she was experiencing due to OCD.

Adoption of the Anti-Inflammatory Diet

Together with a pediatric dietician, Emma and her parents created a customized meal plan that could provide Emma with the desired anti-inflammatory effects through diet. Her nutritional needs were also considered, making diet plans that catered to her preferences. While every type of food was added to provide complete nutrition, sugary drinks, snacks, and processed foods were stopped, as these foods are the main contributors to increasing inflammation.

Although it took several months, Emma and her parents noticed significant improvements in OCD symptoms and overall health.

Reduction in Obsessive Thoughts: The obsessive thoughts that bothered her constantly decreased in intensity and frequency, relieving her from daily stress.

Enhanced Emotional Well-Being: As the OCD symptoms improved, Emma's emotional well-being also improved. She became happier, took challenges with optimism, and was less prone to anxiety and frustration.

Improved School Performance: With a significant decrease in OCD symptoms, Emma's school performance improved exponentially. Her parents and teachers noted her increased engagement in class and improved academic outcomes.

Greater Social Engagement: The emotional stability she achieved allowed her to easily engage in school activities, fostering a bond of relationships with her peers and contributing to her emotional well-being.

Maintaining the Lifestyle

Emma's parents were thrilled with her progress. They opted to sustain the Anti-Inflammatory Diet as a long-term lifestyle choice. They continued to develop exciting and nutritious meals to keep Emma engaged with her diet. They also emphasized the importance of providing her with ongoing support through therapy and techniques for stress management.

Emma's story exemplifies how the Anti-Inflammatory Diet, thoughtfully devised with the guidance of a pediatric dietitian, can be a valuable adjunct to managing childhood OCD. It led to a significant reduction in OCD symptoms, an enhanced emotional state, improved school performance, and a more fulfilling social life. This success story underscores the potential of a balanced and anti-inflammatory approach in supporting the well-being of children living with OCD.

Chapter Takeaways

- The gut-brain axis is a communication system between the gut and the brain.

- The enteric nervous system, central nervous system, immune system, and endocrine system are also involved in the proper functioning of the gut-brain axis.

- Novel approaches like changing diet patterns and using probiotics and prebiotics are being practiced keeping the gut microbiota thriving and mitigate adverse effects on mental health.

- Disruptions in neurotransmitters have been linked to gut-related medical conditions that can ultimately affect mental health.

- Mood disorders and cognitive dysfunction become evident when the gut is inflamed.

- The stress hormones released by the brain can impact the gut function negatively.

- Serotonin is a neurotransmitter that regulates mood, and 90% of it is produced by the enterochromaffin cells in the gut.

- Inflammation, reduction of gut microbiota, disruption in the production of signaling molecules, and anxiety are common problems that affect the gut-brain axis.
- Taking adequate amounts of magnesium in the diet reduces stress, improves signaling, and improves sleep, which positively affects the gut-brain axis.
- An anti-inflammatory diet will eventually improve digestion, strengthen joints, keep blood sugar levels in check, improve heart health, and help massively with weight management.

The next chapter discusses practical ways to craft a personal strategy for your child, tailoring a routine that addresses their specific needs and methods you can implement to track the progress and improve the outcomes.

Chapter 7: Assembling Your Arsenal

"Recovery from OCD is a journey, not a destination. It's about learning to manage your thoughts and behaviors, not eliminating them entirely." – Jonathan Abramowitz

While there's no magic fix for OCD, there are effective treatments available. The best approach to tackling OCD is through cognitive behavioral therapy. CBT helps people change their thinking habits for the better, showing them how to shift from negative thoughts to more positive ones. Since OCD is rooted in obsessive thoughts, CBT can help individuals learn to break free from those endless loops of worrying and focus on other things instead. They can discover ways to deal with those "bad thoughts" without resorting to compulsions. This could involve going for a bike ride, taking a deep breath and counting to five, or even trying out fun activities like drawing or playing with stress relieving toys to stay calm and improve concentration.

To effectively treat OCD, it's essential to tackle all three aspects: the body, thoughts, and behavior. The majority of the therapeutic work should focus on addressing thoughts and behaviors. The treatment process unfolds in a systematic manner, addressing each part in turn. You can start by teaching relaxation and breathing techniques to your child, along with other methods to help the body calm down. Once these strategies are in place, you can move on to addressing the thoughts component. While practicing relaxation and breathing exercises, you will need to introduce techniques to challenge and change harmful thought patterns. As the child continues to work on both relaxation and modifying their thought processes, you should gradually transition into helping them confront their fears through behavioral exposures. This step involves systematically facing the situations or triggers that provoke their OCD-related anxiety.

Addressing the Body Symptoms

A lot of kids with OCD feel anxious in a way that shows up in their bodies. They might seem fidgety, restless, or struggle to unwind, especially at bedtime. So, the first thing to teach your child is how to relax their body and control their breathing to manage stress effectively, and it can also be handy when they're faced with their OCD triggers.

1. Calm Breathing

Have your child lie down on a comfy surface like a yoga mat, bed, floor, or even a soft cushion with a foam or pillow on their upper chest. Then, make them practice breathing slowly in through the nose and out through the mouth. The goal is to let the air travel all the way down to the lower belly, which makes the lower belly gently rise and fall while the foam block on the chest stays still. At first, many children find it tricky to keep the block steady or might push their lower belly out before taking a full breath. So, aim for a slow inhale through the nose for a count of 4 and a slow exhale through the mouth for a count of 6 (it's better if the exhale is longer than the inhale). With some practice, your child will get the hang of it. This natural way of breathing, where the breath goes into the lower belly, is called "lower diaphragmatic breathing."

2. **One-Nostril Breathing**

In this technique, the child holds one nostril closed (with their mouth also closed) and breathes in and out through just one nostril. Start with a slow inhale for a count of 5 and an exhale for a count of 7. Over time, you can increase it to an inhale for 10 and an exhale for 12 or even longer. This kind of breathing helps create a calm feeling, and after doing it for about 5 minutes, it leads to a deep state of relaxation. Make sure you initially try these breathing techniques when the child is already calm. Once they've got the hang of it in a relaxed state, it becomes easier to use these techniques when they're feeling anxious. These breathing strategies are particularly helpful for children with stomach aches or other tummy issues due to anxiety and OCD.

3. Progressive Muscle Relaxation (PMR)

With PMR, the child will have to tighten and hold each muscle group in their body, then let go and relax them. The goal is to recognize when their muscles are tense and quickly release that tension. Starting with their hands, your child should make fists, hold them for 5 seconds, and then let go. They will be able to feel the difference between tense and relaxed muscles. Make them follow this pattern for their hands, arms, shoulders, back, abdomen, legs, feet, and face. Finally, ask them to do it for their entire body all at once. With practice, your child will learn how to relax their body swiftly and let go of any built-up tension. This skill gives them more control over their body's responses when they're anxious.

4. Exercise and Yoga

Moving your body is another great way to release tension and manage anxiety. Doing 20-

30 minutes of cardio exercises every day can be really helpful. It often clears your mind as you work out your body. Yoga is also fantastic for children with OCD. It teaches them to be still and present in the moment, connecting their mind and body. Even starting with a short routine of five yoga poses in 15 minutes is a great start. For example, when a child does a handstand against a wall, they're not thinking about anything else; they're entirely focused on the handstand and feeling what it's like to be fully present in their body. Younger children can enjoy using Yoga Pretzels, which are colorful cards with easy steps to get into various yoga positions. Older children might like watching online videos or trying a teen yoga class.

5. **Meditation**

Lastly, children who learn to meditate experience a unique state of mind where they temporarily let go of their thoughts and just exist in the present moment. With practice, they can reach deeper levels of awareness. There are many apps that teach meditation, and while not all kids may be super into it, introducing them to meditation suggests that they can experience a calmer state when they're not caught up in their thoughts.

The main idea behind all these relaxation techniques is to widen the gap between feeling stressed and feeling relaxed. The more children practice relaxing, the easier it becomes to return to a state of calmness.

Addressing the Thoughts Component

Dealing with the thoughts that come with OCD is a big part of getting better at dealing with the symptoms. The main goal here is to recognize these thoughts as "OCD symptoms" and not real thoughts that deserve attention. When your child starts to see them as OCD, they can start fighting them. However, the problem is that OCD thoughts might seem like regular thoughts even though they're not. Here are some ways to challenge these OCD thoughts:

1. **Loop Recordings**

Think of this as making a recording of the thoughts and worries that plague an OCD mind. Ask your child to write down all their OCD thoughts exactly as they sound in their head, and then record them (using a phone). Ask them to play this recording for about 10-15 minutes every day. This might seem strange because they're listening to their own worries, but it's actually very effective. With repetition, their worries will become less scary and more boring. By hearing their thoughts out loud, it'll be like they're watching them from the outside, and they lose their power.

2. Uncertainty Training Recordings

This is similar to loop recordings, but you turn the OCD thoughts into "uncertainty training" thoughts. For example, if your child worries about getting sick from touching something, they can change it to "It is always possible that I will get sick from touching that." The goal is to learn to be okay with not knowing something for sure. OCD makes people seek certainty, but when they can handle not being sure, it weakens OCD's grip. Here's an example:

Imagine a child named Alex who worries about accidentally hurting animals by stepping on them. Here's how they might do loop and uncertainty training recordings:

- **Alex's Original Thought:**

"What if I hurt an animal when I walk outside? I must wear soft flip-flops to check the bottom for animals. I always talk to my mom about stepping on things at school to make sure I don't hurt any animals. Sometimes, I go back to check, and I avoid playing on the grass or dirt because I'm scared, I'll hurt something. I also worry about a stray cat, so I put out milk for it."

- **Loop Recording by Alex:**

"What if I hurt an animal? What if I hurt something and don't even know it? I should check again. What if there are animals I can't see? What if the cat gets sick because I didn't put out milk?"

- **Uncertainty Training Recording by Alex:**

"It's always possible I might hurt an animal. It's always possible I hurt something without realizing it. I can't know for sure. There might be animals I can't see. It's always possible the cat might get sick because I didn't put out milk."

The point of these recordings is not to make your child feel okay with the bad things they worry about happening. It's about making the thoughts themselves less powerful and less upsetting. No matter what the content of the thoughts is, the idea is to become desensitized to them, which means they won't bother your child as much. When using loop and uncertainty training recordings, sometimes children make several of them. Once a recording feels unalarming and boring, they can stop listening to it and focus on others. However, you shouldn't let them turn these recordings into a new ritual or compulsion. There's a limit to how many additional recordings should be made, usually no more than 5 in total.

3. Positive Self-Talk

Positive self-talk is like having a toolbox of helpful thoughts that your child uses to fight against OCD and avoid compulsions. Unlike the loop and uncertainty recordings, which are used at specific times, self-talk is something your child can use while facing their fears or even in daily life. Here's a list of self-talk statements to help your child reframe their experience with OCD:

- I may feel uneasy, but I can handle it.
- Even though I'm scared, I'm safe.
- Right now, everything is okay. I'm fine.
- I can tolerate the discomfort that comes with facing my OCD.
- These are just OCD thoughts; they don't reflect reality.
- It's the OCD talking; I don't have to pay attention to it.

- How would someone without OCD think and act in this situation?
- It's me versus the OCD. Every time I resist, I get stronger.
- I won't let OCD make decisions for me or my family.
- What's the proactive thing to do here?
- I've never regretted facing my fears or challenging my OCD.
- Thoughts are just thoughts; they have no power unless I give it to them.
- I can observe my thoughts without getting caught up in them.
- I must label these thoughts as OCD symptoms, not real thoughts to consider.
- I can "sit with" and tolerate discomfort; it'll pass.
- Staying with discomfort allows it to fade away.
- I can handle negative emotions; I won't be overwhelmed by them.
- I can tolerate uncertainty; it's a normal part of life.

- Courage comes after facing fears. I can do this.
- I won't let these thoughts control my life. I'm changing how I relate to them.
- Once I label a thought as OCD, it won't bother me. I'm not afraid of it.
- What action can I take right now to connect with something or someone?

This self-talk helps your child challenge and "talk back" to OCD. They can use these statements when dealing with triggers or whenever they need to stand up to their OCD thoughts. Recognizing OCD as something separate from themselves makes it easier for them to fight it.

4. "Stamping" It OCD

Imagine you've identified the different OCD thoughts your child has. Now, take a piece of paper and write some of those thoughts down, leaving some space between each. Next, grab a red Sharpie marker and have your child "stamp" those OCD thoughts by writing "OCD" over them in big, bold letters. When you cover the thought with thick red ink, it becomes hard to read, making it easier to dismiss. Many people find this visual technique helpful. When random OCD thoughts pop up, they visualize "stamping" them with a big "OCD" stamp, helping them let go of these thoughts. The goal here is not to forget the thoughts but to label them as OCD symptoms and dismiss them as irrelevant.

5. Using Distraction

Sometimes, your child might be too worked up to use other techniques, or they could be in the middle of an exposure exercise. That's when distraction becomes handy. It helps your child temporarily shift their focus to something else and then return to the exposure exercise feeling calmer. For example, if your child is bothered by thoughts about a loved one getting hurt and usually does some specific actions like shaking their head or tapping their fingers in response, they need to learn not to perform these compulsions. But just knowing this can trigger anxiety. So, before tackling the real work, a little distraction can calm things down. Distraction engages the mind and gives the body a chance to relax. Here are some distraction techniques:

- Make lists: Names, fruits, cities, or anything else your child can think of.
- List five things related to a category, like favorite books or musicians.

- Play games or puzzles, like word searches.

These distraction techniques should be simple and require minimal effort or materials. They're only meant to be used for a short time before diving into the challenging work of resisting OCD. The reason for this is that your child needs to learn how to handle and endure the discomfort that comes from not engaging in OCD behaviors or rituals. Avoiding those unpleasant feelings is just another form of avoidance and won't help them overcome OCD. They need to become accustomed to these feelings to stop being emotionally triggered by them.

Remember, the ultimate goal is to empower your child to handle and dismiss OCD thoughts effectively, not to let those thoughts control their life. These strategies work together to help them achieve that.

Dealing with the OCD Behavior Component

When someone has OCD, they often show it through certain actions like doing things repeatedly (compulsions), following specific routines (rituals), or avoiding situations that make them anxious. Children with OCD might also seek reassurance a lot, usually from a parent or caregiver, and ask many questions. If a child with OCD can't avoid something that triggers their anxiety, they'll feel distressed and might do a ritual later to make themselves feel better. If they can't do their usual compulsion, they may get upset.

These compulsions and rituals can be easy to spot or quite subtle. Most parents are surprised to find out just how much time and energy their child spends on these actions. It's a cycle: something triggers anxiety, they have certain thoughts, they do the rituals to make the anxiety go away (even though it's only temporary), and this cycle keeps OCD going. In therapy, children are taught that when they don't do the ritual, their anxiety might go up for a bit, but if they keep practicing not doing it, they can overcome OCD. So, they trade short-term relief for long-term freedom. Here's how you can get your child to do that:

1. **Facing Fears**

Children need to learn that it's okay to feel anxious and uncomfortable sometimes, and this is crucial for their recovery. They must face their fears instead of avoiding them. A good way to help is through Exposure/Response Prevention, ERP, to face their fears on purpose. It involves deliberately putting the child in a situation that makes them anxious and then teaching them not to do their usual ritual or compulsion.

The child must learn how to tolerate the discomfort that comes from not doing their rituals. Over time, they'll see that the anxiety goes down, and the urge to do the ritual fades away. This is called habituation, and it's why you can gradually make the exposure exercises longer and harder. When a child realizes they can face their fears and tolerate the anxiety, it boosts their confidence and helps them overcome OCD.

2. Creating a Plan

To start, make a list of the situations that trigger your child's OCD. Then, turn these triggers into specific challenges or "exposures." For example, if a trigger is using public bathrooms, the challenge might be to "walk into a public bathroom and touch the faucet with your hands." Rank these challenges from easiest to hardest and create a ladder with steps on a poster board. Each time your child faces a fear successfully, mark it on the ladder to track their progress. Three crucial things to remember when facing fears are repetition (doing the challenges over and over), frequency (doing them often), and spending enough time in the situations to get used to them (prolonged time).

3. Helpful Mindsets

Teach your child some helpful ways to think about facing their fears. You can tell them that sometimes, they must go through something difficult to get past it. It's like that saying, "We can't go over it, we can't go under it, oh no, we've got to go through it!" Also, explain the difference between being reactive (making decisions based on feelings) and proactive (making decisions based on values). Lastly, use the idea of a "savings account." Every time your child does a ritual, they use up some of their savings, but when they prevent a ritual or face a fear, they save more money. This helps them see their progress.

4. Finding the Right Balance

Sometimes, there are rituals that children can't completely avoid, like washing hands or avoiding allergens. In these cases, set clear rules and times for these behaviors so they don't become excessive or harmful. The goal is to help them regain control over their lives and not let OCD rule them.

Building a Support System

Dealing with your child's OCD can be emotionally draining. A support system, including family, friends, and professionals, will offer a safe space for you to express your feelings, fears, and frustrations. You should also seek professional help for your child from a qualified therapist or psychiatrist.

- **Open Communication:** Talk openly with your partner, family members, and close friends about your child's OCD. Encourage them to ask questions and share their concerns.

- **Support Groups:** Consider joining a local or online support group for parents of children with OCD. These groups provide invaluable advice and a sense of community.

- **Professional Guidance:** Consult with mental health professionals who specialize in OCD. They can provide tailored advice for your family and connect you with resources.

- **School Involvement:** Collaborate with your child's school to create an Individualized Education Plan (IEP) or a 504 Plan that addresses their specific needs related to OCD.

- **Self-Care:** Don't forget to take care of yourself. Your well-being is essential for effectively supporting your child. Engage in self-care activities, and lean on your support system when needed.

Chapter Takeaways

- Effective treatment for OCD involves addressing three components: the body, thoughts, and behavior.

- Relaxation techniques, like deep breathing, one-nostril breathing, progressive muscle relaxation, exercise, yoga, and meditation, help manage physical symptoms of anxiety and OCD.

- Cognitive-behavioral therapy (CBT) is a powerful approach to modify harmful thought patterns and behaviors associated with OCD.

- Visual techniques like "stamping" OCD thoughts can help children label them as symptoms and dismiss them.

- Finding the right balance with rituals that can't be completely avoided is crucial to avoid excessive behaviors and promote independence in children with OCD.

Addressing OCD involves a multifaceted approach. In this chapter, you've explored various strategies, from loop recordings and positive self-talk to "stamping" OCD thoughts and using distraction techniques. Moreover, work on reducing family accommodations to promote progress in managing OCD behaviors. If you keep helicopter parenting, your child will never be able to move forward. So, combine these strategies and tailor them to your child's specific needs, and you will be able to better equip them in their journey to overcome OCD and regain control over their lives. Once you've come up with a suitable plan that's specifically tailored to your child's needs, you'll need to share this with them. How? Read all about it in the next chapter.

Chapter 8: A Compassionate Confrontation

"Understanding is the first step to conquering. The more we know about something, the less scary it becomes." - Fred Rogers

Parenting is a complex and ever-evolving journey filled with moments of joy, challenges, and essential discussions. Among these conversations, discussing Obsessive-Compulsive Disorder (OCD) with your child requires care and sensitivity. Think of it as a compassionate confrontation, and setting the stage for this dialogue is crucial to ensure your child feels understood, supported, and safe.

Opening the dialogue can be challenging, and as a parent, your role in supporting your child through their OCD challenges is pivotal. This chapter highlights strategies that will help you foster an environment where your children feel comfortable sharing their thoughts and experiences.

Sharing the Plan with Your Child

Explaining the Treatment Plan

A compassionate conversation about OCD with your child can only be established if you explain the treatment plan to them clearly and emphatically. It acts as a roadmap towards managing and, in many cases, tackling the challenges posed by OCD. Understanding the treatment plan can be overwhelming for children because they can't fully grasp technical jargon like adults do, and you must communicate that the plan is not a solitary challenge but a collaborative effort between you and your child.

As you consider various treatment options and decide on one, the first step is to tackle the emotional roller coaster you're experiencing. If you feel stressed or worried, reflect on your reaction to the treatment plan with your partner, therapist, or friend. Talking through your thoughts and discussions helps you understand your concerns, and in turn, it helps shape the conversation you'll be having with your child.

Opening the conversation is challenging, and the treatment must be explained in words your child can understand. It's tempting to resort to bedtime stories, and while these explanations can be highly creative and fun, they can also be incorrect. The way you structure a conversation for a preschooler will be different than for a teen. Take a look at various examples to illustrate these age-appropriate conversations.

Talking with Preschoolers

Preschoolers think in concrete terms and understand a conversation better if simple words are used. For example, help them imagine what it feels like when pieces in a puzzle don't fit quite right. It can make them worried and scared, but you have a puzzle solver! Explaining the treatment for OCD is like having a puzzle-solving kit, and it has plenty of fun tools. You can say that it includes talking to a special friend (therapist) who gives helpful hints. The explanation helps your child grasp the concept of OCD and the treatment process in an engaging and relatable way. You don't need to stick with this analogy, and you can form one specific to your situation.

Talking with School-Age Children

School-age children have a better understanding of how the human body and mind work. While the discussion needs to be simple and straightforward, they can easily understand more complicated explanations. You can dive into the specifics of the treatment and explain why they need to visit a therapist and how it will be beneficial.

School-age children typically have low attention spans, so spreading the conversation over a certain period is wise. Consider setting aside a few minutes each day and having an informal discussion. It helps establish a routine, allows your child to ask any follow-up questions, and, most importantly, prevents them from getting overwhelmed.

Talking with Teens

At this age, your children are grown-ups. You'll need to respect and acknowledge this by asking what they want and need to know and following it up with straightforward and honest answers. Unlike younger children, teens are better able to articulate their feelings regarding a certain treatment plan, and it's vital you take their opinions into consideration.

Clarifying Roles and Expectations

As a parent, you may struggle with clearly understanding the role you and your child will play in managing OCD. Think of it as a group project. You'll only succeed if the groundwork for effective collaboration is established.

Discussing Roles

Explicitly discuss roles and acknowledge that your child is at the center of this process. They will actively learn and practice strategies to manage their condition. If at any point they feel overwhelmed or feel as if the techniques being practiced aren't helpful, they're allowed to share their opinion. Your role as a parent is one of support and guidance. You will provide love, understanding, and encouragement throughout the process.

Managing Expectations

Expectations need to be managed beforehand, or you'll find yourself giving vague instructions to your children with little to no effect. Setting realistic expectations for the treatment journey accommodates any challenges you and your child will face. While adults understand that progress is not linear, children may feel overwhelmed when they experience a setback. A conversation emphasizing that the treatment plan isn't an immediate fix will go a long way. Encourage patience and perseverance, emphasizing that you and your child are committed to effectively managing OCD.

Initiating the Conversation

Initiating a conversation about OCD with your child is a sensitive step, and choosing the right time and setting will impact its effectiveness. Here are some considerations to keep in mind:

Timing

Choose a moment when you can dedicate your full attention to the discussion and ensure ample time for follow-up questions. It can be challenging if you've got a packed schedule, but choose a time that works for you, your partner, and your child. Don't initiate the conversation during stressful moments such as exam season or when your child is busy with other activities. Once you agree on a time, look at where it will occur.

Setting

Creating an environment of trust and openness is essential, and it can be achieved by choosing a comfortable, non-threatening, and familiar setting. This can be your study room, cozy living room corner, or any place you share with your child to talk, relax, and unwind.

Before initiating the conversation, let your child know you want to have a special, private conversation with them. If they're habitual to getting anxious, assure them they've done nothing wrong, and they're allowed to share their thoughts and feelings without judgment and pressure. Encourage them to express themselves honestly, and instead of keeping all the questions until the very end, allow them to engage and ask questions whenever they have a concern as the conversation progresses.

Starting the Dialogue

Opening a dialogue about OCD, especially with children, can be daunting. The discussion requires the right words and a sensitive and empathetic approach. Take a look at how you can open the conversation and build upon it.

Express Your Concern

The first step is to establish the goal of the conversation. Initiate by expressing your love and concern. For example, you can begin with, "I've noticed that you've been dealing with some challenging thoughts and behaviors lately, and I want you to know I'm here to support you." This assures your child that you're attentive, understand the problem, and are ready to provide the help and resources they need.

Steering the Conversation

You must set the conversation's course by recognizing and labeling what your child has been experiencing. Delicately introduce OCD, and don't assume any knowledge on your child's end. You can say, "You know, what you've been going through lately, it's called OCD. It's important to understand that." A simple dialogue helps gently introduce the topic of OCD and opens the door for further discussion.

Ways to Discuss OCD

Communicating the concept of OCD, especially to young children, requires a thoughtful and simplified approach. Here, you'll learn various strategies to simplify complex ideas by looking at different scenarios.

Use Simple Language

Imagine sitting down with your child who's been showing signs of repetitive behaviors like excessive hand washing. You gently say, "Sometimes, our brains make us want to do things repeatedly, like washing our hands. It's okay, and we can learn to control it together." Using plain language and avoiding jargon makes the concept accessible to their young minds.

Metaphors for Clarity

Metaphors are handy tools to simplify hard-to-understand concepts. Picture a scenario where your child feels compelled to count objects repeatedly. In technical jargon, it is described as a stuck thought loop. However, you can explain that it's like a hamster running on a wheel inside your head, and sometimes it's hard to make the hamster stop, and it keeps going in circles until it gets tired. This imaginative image helps your child visualize the concept of repetitive thoughts and behaviors.

Storytelling to Relate

Stories keep children occupied for hours, and with a bit of creativity, you'll be able to customize just about any story to help your child relate to the character's experiences. For instance, tell them the story about Alex.

Alex experiences worries about cleanliness and often finds himself getting stuck on thoughts about germs and how he feels better after washing his hands. One day, Alex's school had a special picnic at a beautiful park, and he was excited to join his friends for a day of fun. But as soon as he arrived and saw the lush green grass and the picnic tables, his worries about cleanliness began to creep in.

Alex knew that the picnic area was usually quite clean, but his mind started to race with thoughts about invisible germs lurking everywhere. He was torn between enjoying the day with his friends and the need to wash his hands.

His best friend, Lily, noticed that something was bothering Alex and asked him what was wrong. Alex hesitated but then decided to share his concerns with her. Lily was a kind and understanding friend. She told him, "I understand that you worry about germs, but I promise you, we'll take good care of each other today. And when it's time to eat, we can all wash our hands together."

Alex felt a sense of relief, knowing that he had a supportive friend by his side. As the day went on, he played games, laughed, and had a fantastic time. And when it was time to eat, just as Lily had promised, they all washed their hands together before enjoying a delicious picnic lunch.

Throughout the day, Alex learned that even when worries about cleanliness and germs tried to get in the way of his fun, he could still have a great time with the help of understanding friends and by taking sensible precautions.

Through Alex's story, your child will relate to the character's experiences and begin to understand OCD as a common challenge.

Visual Aids

Visual aids can be a powerful tool when explaining the concept of thought loops associated with OCD to a child. Take a piece of paper and draw a simple track or path in the shape of a circle. Inside the circle, write "Germs" as the recurring thought. Explain that this thought keeps going around in their head, like a race car on a circular track. To make it more engaging, you can use colorful toys or objects. Find a toy car, preferably one that stands out with vibrant colors. Place the car on the circular path, representing the thought of germs. Roll the car around the path and explain that it's as if their mind is stuck in this loop, always coming back to thinking about germs. Introduce the idea of breaking the thought loop. Use a separate object, like a traffic cone or a "stop" sign, to represent ways to interrupt the loop. Show how the thought can be redirected or stopped by placing the object in the path of the car or thought of germs.

Role-Playing for Engagement

Imagine a scenario where you and your child engage in role-playing. You pretend to be a character in a story. In this story, one character has OCD, and they constantly check if the lights are off. You can demonstrate how this behavior might make the character feel stuck and anxious. Role-playing helps your child understand how certain behaviors can become repetitive and distressing.

Repetition with Reinforcement

Children learn through repetition. Repeating explanations and reassurances about OCD regularly can reinforce their understanding. You might say, "Remember, sometimes our brains can get stuck on certain thoughts. But we can learn to make those thoughts go away together." This repetition helps solidify the concept in their minds.

Facing Resistance

Understanding why your child might resist discussing or accepting their OCD is critical to providing adequate support. You need to approach this resistance with empathy and patience while normalizing their feelings of discomfort.

Why Your Child Might Resist

Fear of Judgment

Your child may be concerned that if they talk about their OCD, others will judge them. The fear of being seen as different or "weird" can be overwhelming, especially for children who are likely to seek peer acceptance and approval.

Shame and Embarrassment

OCD-related thoughts and behaviors can be deeply embarrassing. Your child may feel ashamed of their compulsions or intrusive thoughts, which can make discussing them a daunting prospect.

Lack of Understanding

Children may not fully grasp what OCD is or why they experience it. This lack of comprehension can lead to resistance because they may not know how to articulate their feelings or experiences.

Desire for Normalcy

Many children aspire to fit in and be perceived as "normal." They may resist discussing OCD because they worry it sets them apart from their peers, potentially making them feel isolated.

Anxiety

It's essential to recognize that OCD comes with high anxiety levels. Discussing their symptoms can be anxiety-inducing, which may contribute to your child's reluctance to engage in the conversation.

Normalizing Their Feelings of Discomfort

Validate Their Feelings

Begin by validating your child's emotions. Let them know that it's entirely normal to feel uncomfortable or worried when discussing something as personal as OCD. Say something like, "It's completely okay to feel a bit uneasy when talking about something like OCD."

Provide Reassurance

Reassure your child that you're there to support them unconditionally. Make it clear that you won't judge or criticize them. Reiterate your commitment to facing this challenge together, saying, "We're a team, and we'll tackle this together."

Emphasize Commonality

Explain that many people, both children and adults, experience OCD. Share stories or examples of well-known individuals or fictional characters who have faced similar challenges. This can help your child understand they are not alone in this journey.

Encourage Small Steps

Suggest taking small, manageable steps when discussing OCD. Your child can start by sharing a little bit about their experiences and gradually open up more as they become more comfortable. Encourage them to go at their own pace.

Professional Help

If resistance persists and is causing significant distress, consider involving a mental health professional specializing in OCD. They can provide strategies and support tailored to your child's needs, helping them navigate their resistance more effectively.

Setting Achievable Goals

Setting achievable goals for your child's progress in managing OCD is a pivotal part of their journey to recovery and improved well-being. These goals should be well-defined, attainable, and tailored to your child's unique circumstances. Here's a detailed guide on how to effectively set and celebrate these milestones while providing a deeper understanding of each aspect:

Setting Realistic Goals

Assess Your Child's Current Situation

Begin by conducting a thorough assessment of your child's OCD. Identify specific behaviors, intrusive thoughts, or compulsions that are causing distress or interfering with their daily life. Understanding the current challenges is the foundation for setting meaningful goals.

Break Down Goals into Manageable Steps

Addressing OCD can be overwhelming, so break larger objectives into smaller, more manageable steps. For instance, if your child struggles with time-consuming hand-washing rituals, an initial goal might be to reduce the time spent washing hands by a certain percentage. This incremental approach allows for steady progress.

Ensure Goals Are Specific and Measurable

Say your child has OCD-related compulsions related to arranging their belongings in a specific order before leaving the house. A vague goal might be, "Let's try to be less organized." However, this goal lacks clarity and measurability.

Instead, you can set a specific and measurable goal like, "Reduce the time spent arranging belongings before leaving the house from 30 minutes to 15 minutes." This goal is clear, as it specifies the compulsive behavior (arranging belongings) and the desired change (reducing time). It's also measurable because you can track the time spent on this task and compare it to the set target.

By setting a clear and measurable goal, you and your child can easily understand what needs to be achieved, and progress can be monitored effectively. It transforms a vague aspiration into a concrete objective, making it more attainable and actionable.

Consider the Timeline

Recognize that progress in managing OCD may not always be linear, and setbacks can occur. Establish a flexible timeline for achieving each goal, allowing for adjustments and modifications along the way. Flexibility is essential to accommodate any challenges that may arise.

Celebrating Achievements

Acknowledge Small Wins

Celebrate even the smallest steps toward the goal. These milestones represent progress and effort. Acknowledge and praise your child for their dedication, reinforcing their motivation and self-esteem.

Use Positive Reinforcement

Positive reinforcement is a powerful tool for managing your child's OCD. When they successfully complete a goal, such as reducing their compulsions, acknowledge and celebrate their achievement. This recognizes their hard work and motivates them to continue their progress. Consider offering verbal praise, expressing your pride in their efforts and determination. Small rewards or treats can serve as tangible tokens of recognition, celebrating their accomplishments and boosting their self-esteem. These positive reinforcement strategies create a supportive and encouraging environment, helping your child build confidence and resilience in their journey towards managing OCD.

Maintain a Progress Journal

Keep a journal to document your child's achievements and milestones. This journal will be a visual record of their progress, providing motivation and reminding them of how far they've come in their journey.

Involve the Support System

Encourage friends and family to celebrate your child's achievements as well. Their support and acknowledgment will boost your child's confidence and create a sense of unity in their support system.

Set New Goals

After successfully reaching a goal, collaborate with your child to develop new, challenging yet attainable objectives. This continuous cycle of goal setting and celebration maintains momentum and progress throughout the treatment process.

Chapter Takeaways

Opening the Dialogue

- Initiating a conversation about OCD with your child requires care and sensitivity.
- Setting the stage for a compassionate confrontation is crucial for your child to feel understood, supported, and safe.

Sharing the Treatment Plan

- Explain the treatment plan to your child clearly and emphatically.
- Emphasize that managing OCD is a collaborative effort between you and your child.
- Reflect on your emotional reactions to the treatment plan and seek support from your partner, therapist, or friend to better shape the conversation with your child.

Age-Appropriate Conversations

- Tailor your conversation style to your child's age and developmental stage.
- Use simple language and relatable analogies for preschoolers.
- Explain the treatment specifics and benefits for school-age children, spreading the conversation over time.

- Engage teens with straightforward and honest discussions, respecting their opinions and feelings.

Clarifying Roles and Expectations

- Establish roles clearly, with your child at the center of the process.
- Encourage your child to share their thoughts and concerns throughout the treatment journey.
- Set realistic expectations, emphasizing that progress may not be immediate and requires patience and perseverance.

Initiating the Conversation

- Choose a dedicated time for the discussion, free from distractions and stress.
- Create a comfortable, non-threatening setting to foster trust and openness.
- Assure your child that they've done nothing wrong and can express themselves without judgment or pressure.

Starting the Dialogue

- Express your love and concern to establish the conversation's goal.
- Delicately introduce OCD, assuming no prior knowledge on your child's part.

- Open the door for further discussion by recognizing and labeling your child's experiences.

Ways to Discuss OCD

- Simplify complex ideas with plain language for young children.
- Use metaphors to help visualize OCD-related concepts.
- Customize stories to relate to your child's experiences and normalize OCD.
- Utilize visual aids and role-playing for engagement.
- Reinforce understanding through repetition and reassurance.

Facing Resistance

- Understand potential reasons for your child's resistance, such as fear of judgment, shame, lack of understanding, desire for normalcy, or anxiety.
- Normalize their feelings of discomfort and validate their emotions.
- Provide reassurance that you're there to support them unconditionally.
- Emphasize the commonality of OCD experiences to reduce isolation.

- Encourage small steps and consider involving a mental health professional if resistance persists.

Setting Achievable Goals

- Assess your child's current OCD challenges to lay the foundation for meaningful goals.

- Break down goals into manageable, specific, and measurable steps.

- Establish a flexible timeline to accommodate setbacks.

- Celebrate achievements, even small wins, to motivate continued progress.

- Use positive reinforcement, including verbal praise and tangible rewards, to recognize your child's efforts.

- Maintain a progress journal to track their journey visually.

- Involve the support system, including friends and family, in celebrating achievements.

- Continue the cycle of setting new goals to maintain momentum and progress throughout treatment.

Remember that your child's journey with OCD is a collaborative effort. Approach each conversation with love, patience, and empathy. By setting achievable goals, offering positive reinforcement, and normalizing their feelings, you can help your child effectively manage OCD and provide them with the support they need to thrive. Facing resistance can be challenging, and you'll learn more about it in the following chapter. It discusses a variety of ways to accommodate emotional outbursts and will equip you with the skills to navigate setbacks.

Chapter 9: Braving the Storm

"Every storm runs out of rain, just like every dark night turns into day." – Gary Allan

You have let your child know what they are suffering from, explained in detail about OCD, and even charted out the treatment procedures you will collectively undergo. Despite all your explanations and assurances, did they respond in a way you didn't expect? For instance, did they lash out at you, try desperately to prove you wrong, or storm off in a fit of rage? In this chapter, you will learn how to handle these outbursts and help bring their emotions under control.

Addressing Difficult Responses

When you first tell your child that they have OCD, their initial reaction may not be too extreme. They might feel curious or concerned about their condition and, at times, afraid of how it might be affecting them. Once you have cleared all their concerns, fears, and doubts, it is then that their repressed emotions may start bubbling up, waiting to overflow like a dormant volcano ready to erupt.

These extreme thoughts, emotions, and responses can occur anytime during the treatment. They may even lead to setbacks in the process, making your child experience their compulsions again. Hence, it is critical to address those difficult responses right away instead of letting them run their course.

Emotional Outbursts

Imagine that your child is calmly playing with their toys. Out of the blue, they start crying uncontrollably. You rush to their aid, thinking they might have hurt themselves on some sharp edge of the toy. You examine them and find that they are in perfect physical health, but they are still bawling their eyes out for some reason. This is what an emotional outburst looks like, and it is associated with OCD. The most common emotion in OCD is anger.

You may have come across your child displaying fits of rage or extreme frustration (teeth-grinding anger and hair-pulling irritation), even when nothing seemed to have set them off. These 'anger attacks' aren't uncommon in OCD. One moment, your child may be as calm as a millpond, and the next, they may be fuming with rage for no apparent reason.

Why Emotional Outbursts Happen and How to Respond

Research shows that nearly half the people suffering from OCD are prone to anger attacks. They have a tendency to shout, threaten, or act aggressively toward others. There could be many causes for these emotional outbursts.

- **Stress and Anxiety:** OCD isn't easy to live with, and its treatment can put pressure on your little one. Since there is no set duration in which the condition can be cured, it leads to stress and anxiety among the patients. This pressure may keep building up, and there will come a time when it becomes too much to bear. That is when they would snap.

  Does your child feel like you don't understand enough about their condition? Maybe their peers are bullying or teasing them about it. Is the child's teacher not taking their OCD into account while teaching? Any one of these instances could add to the already mounting pressure, leading to an emotional outburst.

- **Failing to Contain Obsessions and Compulsions**: As you might know by now, an OCD-affected child's world revolves around their intrusive thoughts and compulsions. As their treatment progresses, they may feel like they aren't able to control their obsessions or keep their compulsions in check. That failure may keep eating them up on the inside until their mind isn't able to hold its weight any longer. They need to unload the weight in some manner, and the easiest way is to release it in a burst of anger or an overwhelming display of frustration.

- **Failed Expectations**: Your child may have set a few expectations for themselves over the course of the treatment, like reducing their intrusive thoughts by half within eight sessions. If they are unable to meet their expectations or goals, especially the simplest ones, then it may lead to anger attacks.

- **Side-effects of Medication**: OCD medications are focused on improving the mental health of the patient, like activating select chemical signals within the brain to reduce compulsive behavior. However, since the human brain is a complex set of responses rapidly interacting with each other, it's hard not to experience any side effects of the medicines. Your child's brain's amygdala (which relates to their emotions) can be affected by OCD medication, leading to emotional outbursts.

- **Interruptions:** Is your child doing a compulsion activity, and do you interrupt them? It may cause them to lash out. Since that emotional outburst was caused because of you, it may create a prolonged rift between you and your child, which could not be easily resolved.

These OCD-related emotional outbursts not only strain interpersonal relationships but may also cause mental and physical harm to your child and those around them. The important point is to not escalate those outbursts. Never tell them flat out, "Don't be angry," or start criticizing their actions.

If they aren't being violent and destructive, let their anger run its course. If not, then let them know that you understand their outburst and can relate to their problems. Be a calming presence instead of an aloof parent. Narrate a positive experience or sing them a soothing song. Once they calm down, hold them close and let them know that you care.

The good news is no matter the reasons for the outburst, they can be managed and brought under control. ERP therapy does most of the work, but you, as a parent, can help out by teaching your child the following activities.

- **The Act of Breathing:** The simple act of focusing on your breathing can take care of many of your mental problems. You need to ask your child to practice these steps for at least five minutes every day.

1. Sit in a place free of distractions. Be as comfortable as you can.
2. Breathe normally and focus on nothing but your breathing process for a while.
3. Now, take a deep breath, hold for five seconds, breathe out, and again hold for five seconds.
4. Continue this cycle for at least five minutes.

   The slower you breathe, the lower your heart rate will be. That will lower the amount of stress hormones in your blood. Thus, if your child focuses on their act of slow breathing during an emotional outburst, their anger and frustration will gradually be reduced and eventually disappear.

- **The Art of Introspection**: Introspection is the process of analyzing your thoughts and assessing your emotions. It helps examine the anger attack from the inside out to be able to deal with it better. Once you teach the art of introspection to your child, they will learn to control their bouts of rage and frustration on their own.

1. Introspection can be done anywhere, but it's best to start off in a familiar place where your child feels safe, like your house.
2. Pick a time when there are the least distractions. Choose a slow afternoon or a silent night.
3. Ask your child to start off with the aforementioned breathing exercise.
4. Tell them to think back on their most recent emotional outburst. It's essential that they are perfectly calm when you tell them this. Otherwise, they may revert back to their agitated state.
5. Ask them what they were feeling. Was it rage, frustration, depression, fear, or something else?
6. Ask them what made them feel that way. They will first state the immediate reason, like interruption during compulsion activity.
7. Prompt them to dig deeper for more reasons.
8. Ask them to think about how they could find solutions to those problematic reasons. Help them reach those solutions if you can.

One of the solutions should be to start introspecting soon after your child has an emotional outburst. This will eventually enable them to control their emotions on their own.

- **The Method of Distraction:** OCD-affected individuals are more focused than normal people. That is sometimes not a good thing, especially during an anger attack. They are so focused on their anger that they ignore anything else that goes on around them. Therefore, distractions are helpful. Teach them how to distract themselves during an emotional outburst. Here are a few solutions.

- Listen to calming music or watch a movie that brings you peace.
- Start reading an inspiring book.
- Walk around the neighborhood.
- Eat something you love.

Navigating Setbacks

Managing emotional outbursts is a part of your child's OCD recovery process. But what about setbacks? Are they common during the treatment? Can your child recover from some major setback? Yes, they can. Before you learn how to navigate setbacks, you need to understand what they are.

Setbacks during OCD treatment could be any action or mental state that your child reverts back to. Assume that they haven't had a hand-washing compulsion for a week. On the eighth day, they suddenly feel the urge to wash their hands from time to time. That is considered a setback. However, did you know that not all setbacks are bad?

There are good setbacks, too, and there are bad setbacks that can be used to your child's advantage. Take the previous hand-washing compulsion example again. Don't try to handle that setback right away. Wait and watch what they do. Are they trying to find a way around the compulsion, like distracting themselves by reading a book? That makes it a good setback! They have learned to adapt to their compulsive behavior, which marks definite progress in their treatment.

If your child has had a bad setback, remember that it isn't permanent. They can get over it and move forward.

Strategies to Regain Momentum

Any bad setback can prove to be a learning experience for your child. They have the capability to transform it into a beneficial setback, and you can help them see it that way.

- **A Wake-up Call:** Most of your child's OCD treatment is homework. They need to keep implementing the skills prescribed by their therapist day in and day out. They would have developed a routine, which may seem cumbersome to them at times. It may cause them to skip a few exercises and skill implementations over time. That is when a setback acts as a wake-up call. It's like a gas station for your car in the middle of nowhere, an oasis at the center of a desert. It will give your child a second wind to try and be free of OCD. Rest assured; they will work doubly hard in implementing their prescribed skills after a setback.

- **A Reflective Period:** Since OCD treatment is a long and uncertain process, it can be tiring to keep track of your child's progress. You may feel like they have made little progress in a long time. But a setback reminds you and your child of the value of that little progress. It's a temporary breather on an infinite journey, a time they can look back on their struggles and reflect on how far they have come. It gives you and your child the courage to go even further to embrace an OCD-free life.

- **A Glitch in the Matrix:** A setback is nothing but a glitch in the matrix of your child's treatment, something that can be fixed. It doesn't mean that they are going backward on their journey, heading back to their OCD-governed life. Let your child know that the setback is nothing but a temporary hurdle, a hitchhiker who will depart at the next stop. Assure them that they don't need to start from scratch. They can continue their journey from the point they left it at before the setback. They simply need to jump over that hurdle to reach the other side and keep going.

Coping with Intrusive Thoughts

As you might know by now, intrusive thoughts are recurring negative thoughts that haunt your child from time to time. They may be reminders of some traumatic event in their past, mental images of experiencing an embarrassing incident, or anything in between. These intrusive thoughts may often circle around many children, be they normal or abnormal. But OCD-affected kids are most prone to them.

There is no need to worry, however. You, as a parent, can help your child cope with those intrusive thoughts. But before you do that, you need to determine whether the thought is indeed intrusive or negatively obsessive.

- If your child is calm and composed by nature, then their intrusive thoughts could be especially chaotic and violent.
- Is it disturbing their mental health, pushing away their positive emotions?
- Are they finding the thought difficult to manage?
- Is it transforming their serene mental state into a turbulent concoction of negative emotions? In short, are they displaying extreme emotions to the smallest of problems?

Once you know that intrusive thoughts have taken hold of your child, you need to follow these basic steps.

1. **Make Them Realize Its Intrusive Nature**: You may have recognized that thought's intrusive nature, but your child hasn't. Explain why their thought is intrusive and help them understand what makes it decidedly negative. They may find it natural to lash out violently but let them know how it adversely affects the people around them and how it infects their mental well-being.

2. **Make Them Accept:** Once your child has understood that an intrusive, negative thought is haunting them, their first instinct

will be to try and fight it. Don't let them fight it, not yet. They first need to accept their obsession so that they can effectively deal with it later. When they try to fight it without accepting the thought, they may end up bruised. Your role is to prepare them for the inevitable battle and make them ready to win.

3. **No Judgments:** Accepting their intrusive thoughts doesn't automatically make your child gain control over them. Make sure they don't judge themselves based on those thoughts. Do they feel different because they imagine hurting their bullies? Does worrying about catching an infection make them feel small? Do they think that unintentionally spreading infections would make them a bad person? Assure them that it is normal behavior.

The following exercises will enable you to help your child cope with their intrusive thoughts more effectively.

- **<u>Meditation</u>**

Meditation is focusing on your breathing, something you learned earlier in this chapter. To help your child cope with their intrusive thoughts, you need to delve into the advanced, more complex concepts of meditation.

1. Start by telling your child to focus on their breathing. Breathe in, breathe out. Hold for five or more seconds between each in and out process.
2. Every time your child inhales, ask them to imagine sucking in all the positivity around them, like a reverse vacuum cleaner that sucks the good things instead of the dirt.
3. Let them relish the positivity for a few seconds.
4. Ask them to focus on their intrusive thoughts and let them imagine blowing them all out as they exhale, like a duckling cleaning its nostrils in bubbles in a pond.
5. Let them hold their breath and cherish that feeling of cleanliness as they become free of their obsession.

Those intrusive thoughts will reform again as your child breathes in the second time, but with each satisfying exhale, a part of those thoughts will relinquish its hold on them. Ask them to practice meditation every day to experience its long-term benefits.

- **<u>Words Have Power</u>**

Remember, intrusive thoughts are temporary manifestations of your child's negative emotions. The key word here is "temporary".

Every temporary thing has a beginning and an end. Your child needs to understand this fact. Whenever any intrusive thoughts haunt their mind, ask them to chant some words that make them realize the impermanence of those thoughts. Something as specific as, "My thoughts won't last long," to something as general as, "This is temporary," works!

- **Visualization**

This is similar to focusing on words, but it requires more imagination. You need to make your child visualize their intrusive thoughts as a temporary part of something permanent. Take the night sky as a permanent entity. A shooting star that streaks across the shimmering blackness can personify their intrusive thoughts. It lasts for but a moment until it vanishes forever.

Alternatively, in the sunlit sky, their intrusive thoughts could be fleeting clouds. At the break of dawn, the passing mist could portray their obsession. You simply need to create a relatable phenomenon for your child to imagine, something with a permanent part of their positive subconscious, along with a temporary personification of their intrusive behavior.

Chapter Takeaways

All in all, while coping with your child's intrusive thoughts, you need to help them focus on their positive emotions. Their ERP treatment will take care of the rest.

- Once your child realizes they have OCD, they may respond in extreme ways.

- These extreme ways or difficult responses include emotional outbursts, progressive setbacks, and giving in to intrusive thoughts.

- Emotional outbursts can be tackled with introspection breathing and distraction exercises.

- Progressive setbacks are just that, progressive. You only need to make your child realize their benefits.

- Finally, intrusive thoughts can be made less intrusive via meditation, visualization, and motivational prompts.

It might make you wonder, what after your child's emotional outbursts, setbacks, and intrusive behavior have been brought under control? What happens when their OCD treatment is over and done with? Their journey of becoming OCD-free doesn't end there. The next chapter explores all the options that you can choose for your child to better cope with their post-treatment problems.

Chapter 10: Navigating Forward

"You don't have to control your thoughts. You just have to stop letting them control you." – Dan Millman.

You, as a parent, would be overjoyed to know that your child has completed their OCD treatment course and has learned to manage the disorder. Your child may not exactly be jumping for joy, however. You need to understand that their compulsions have been with them for most of their life. Whenever they felt sad, performing a ritual cheered them up. When angry or frustrated, it helped calm them down. For them, it was a ship anchored firmly in the raging storm. The mundane regularity of it made them feel safe and secure regardless of what was going on around them.

Performing compulsions used to be a way of life for your child. It was a habit that may be hard to let go of post-treatment. They may begin to miss it and even long for it as time goes by. They don't have the assurance of a solid, dependable scientific treatment anymore. They will need you now more than ever. This chapter will show you how to help your child navigate forward after treatment, how they can maintain their momentum, prepare for adulthood, and find solace among the right group of people.

Preparing for Tomorrow

Facing tomorrow can be a harrowing prospect for your child. They may have gone through today somehow, but they have no idea what is going to come next. So far, OCD was a dependable crutch. It's time for you to take its place.

Let your child know what they can expect going forward. Since they have stepped into an OCD-free life, not unlike yours, describe a normal day in your life to them, every little thing you did, from brushing your teeth in the morning to collapsing on the bed after a hard day's work. Encourage them to tell you how they are feeling at regular intervals.

Assure them that you will be with them through this difficult time, that you understand what they are facing, and that you would like to carry the weight of the burden with them. Encourage them to talk to you about any problems they may face in the future, especially when they get the urge to perform compulsions. Help them identify their ambitions and goals and show them ways in which they could achieve them. Be their life and career guide.

Monitor your child's behavior for any flare-ups or potential relapse. Remember, there is no set time period for an OCD relapse to occur. They may start experiencing their urges within days of the treatment or after many years. More importantly, don't stop their medications without their doctor's recommendation, even if they haven't had an episode in a long time. They might just experience the urge after stopping the medicine.

Maintaining Momentum

Imagine you are lumbering around in the desert, the sun beating down on your bare face, your dry lips screaming for water, but your parched throat can barely get a croak out. The map in your hand clearly shows that a small town is a few miles ahead, but you see nothing on the horizon yet. There are endless plains of barren land all around, except when you look behind you.

Back there, you can faintly notice a vast stretch of water, like a still lake. It doesn't seem too far off. You can possibly reach there in a few good strides. It glimmers from the reflected light of the sun; it calls out to you. You long to bathe in its waters, wash away your exhaustion. However, the world has told you it's nothing but a mirage, a trick of the light. You also know that to be true. Nevertheless, the urge to go back there is strong, much stronger than moving forward into nothingness.

That is exactly the kind of dilemma that OCD patients are faced with post-treatment every single day. Your child is still battling with the urge to relapse into their compulsions, where they feel safe and comfortable. The road ahead is uncertain, but the one behind is familiar. They may have gotten into the habit of keeping their obsessions at bay, but they need to maintain that momentum, lest they fall back into the comforting arms of their previous habits.

OCD compulsions and obsessions cannot be stopped within a day. It's a long process, and your child needs to be motivated to stick to that process throughout. You need to motivate them to continue maintaining their momentum.

- **Give Them a Reward**

Say your child maintained their momentum for a week. That's a fine achievement, given their state of mind. Give them something they have always wanted, like a toy or a game subscription. Did they manage to stay OCD-free for three months straight? Upgrade their reward to a bike or a Virtual Reality (VR) headset. Has it been a year since their last obsessive episode? Upgrade it further to a gaming console or a drone. Any kind of reward is a great motivation for children.

- **Set Goals for Compulsion**

Your child is perfectly capable of handling their compulsions and obsessions post-treatment, but goals imply that they have something to work toward. It also ensures they don't overburden themselves while maintaining their momentum. Set a few achievable goals for their compulsions. For example, if it's an obsession, they have to do it in moderation every day (like in contamination OCD), say handwashing, then give them an initial target of 15 hand washes per day. Keep reducing the number each week. The average human doesn't need to wash their hands more than six to eight times each day, so bring their compulsion down to that number.

- **The Opposite Game**

Whenever your child feels like they need to do something out of fear or anxiety, they need to do the exact opposite of that. Take the hand-washing example again. When they feel like washing their hands, tell them to ask themselves what is making them feel that way.

If the answer is fear of getting contaminated, then tell them to do the exact opposite. Let them get contaminated! Nothing too extreme, though. Just let them play in the rain or snow, build mud castles, roll around in your backyard, etc.

- **Try Once, Try Twice, Try Again**

OCD treatment consists of many trial-and-error methods. Even while determining your child's medication, the doctors could have prescribed several trial medicines before settling for the right drugs and dosage. The process of recovery post-treatment is similar. If your child has performed a compulsion once, ask them to try not to do it again. Have they done it twice? Tell them to try and avoid doing it the third time, and so on. This way, they will know when they have peaked their momentum or minimized their compulsions.

Ensuring Continued Progress Post Treatment

Is your child maintaining their OCD-free momentum? Great work! At the same time, you need to focus on their progress as well. Keep track of their progress so that they will know how far they have come, which will motivate them to continue to improve. Here are a few good tips to ensure a steady rise in their progress graph after treatment.

- **Prepare for the Unexpected:** Make your child aware that just because their treatment is over doesn't mean that there isn't any chance of a relapse. Don't put the fear of relapse into them. Let them know casually and assure them there is no need to worry. It's a common occurrence, and it may happen at any time. Moreover, prepare them for the possibility that their relapsing compulsion may not be the same as before. For example, if they were obsessed with handwashing before treatment, they may feel the urge to hoard old and useless things this time around.

- **Give Free Rein to Their Thoughts**: Ask your child not to block their thoughts, be they harmless or intrusive. Preventing or suppressing the act of thinking will only give rise to more thoughts, and those thoughts may be even more severely intrusive. Let them think whatever they want. If they are intrusive thoughts, it will hone their ability to control their urges. They will try harder to maintain their momentum, which will definitely benefit them in the long run.

- **Don't Let Them Compare**: OCD treatment affects people differently. Some may be cured within months; others may take years to get rid of their obsessions. If your child has a friend who has undergone the same treatment, advise them to talk about anything else but their OCD progress. This not-comparing tip is beneficial for every other part of your child's life, but it's doubly important with OCD recovery.

- **Don't Let Them Avoid Their Fears:** Is that nagging obsessive anxiety or fear crawling out of some dark hole in your child's mind? Their first instinct will be to run away from it and shut it out completely. Don't let them do that. They need to face their fears head-on to overcome them. Running away will only suppress their fears, only to resurface some other time more strongly. Facing their anxieties may put a strain on their momentum, and it may even cause them to relapse for a while, but they have the potential to deal with that fear and relapse and ensure it doesn't occur again.

Preparing for Adulthood

Research has shown that OCD becomes more severe with age. Don't let your child know this just yet because it may become another one of their obsessive anxieties. The age of 10-12 years is when their symptoms may noticeably surface. By the age of 17, they would have become very severe if left untreated.

If you are starting your child's treatment after 17, then studies have shown that it may take more than 10 years for their symptoms to abate. OCD remission (cure) was observed after the age of 30, so your child's adolescent and post-adolescent years would probably be marred by their compulsions and obsessions.

Transitioning to Teen and Adult Years

The earlier you treat your child, the better it will be for their adulthood. The older they get, the harder it will be for them to remember exactly when their OCD began, which may make the doctor's job of prescribing the right medication and treatment all the more difficult. In short, their transition from childhood to adulthood becomes easier if they have treated their OCD early on. To treat it early, you need to recognize it early.

Your child may not recognize intrusive thoughts for what they are. They may think that their compulsive behaviors are a protective cocoon keeping the negativity at bay. They may believe that if they break out of it, the negativity will consume them. Furthermore, they may assume that their obsessions are abnormal, something that may make them look crazy. Hence, they won't tell them about it to you or anyone else.

However, as your child grows up, they will slowly begin to understand the absurdity of hiding their intrusive thoughts. Their growing independence won't let them perceive it as a protective cocoon anymore but as a superstitious belief. They may still think that their obsessions are abnormal, but they will have the sense to address that abnormality by sharing it with someone.

In essence, don't worry at all if you aren't able to detect OCD early on in your child. Late detection may take a longer time for treatment, but they will know exactly why they are getting it treated in the first place. Self-realization paves the way for a more effective treatment procedure.

Finding Support Groups

In an earlier chapter, you learned that you should not let your child compare their progress with others. Isn't that what OCD support groups do, you may wonder? Definitely not. Won't it be natural for your child to compare after listening to the progress of others? For your child, yes, which is why support groups aren't recommended for children under 18 years of age. Invariably, these groups discourage any form of comparison among themselves.

That said, there are several benefits of joining an OCD support group.

- They help your child realize they are not alone. OCD is not as common as you think (only around 1% of the world population has it).
- Your child can find comfort in the similar struggles others have faced.
- They can find hope in the recovery journey of others.
- They can expand their knowledge about OCD.
- Groups help deal with the milder forms of compulsions and obsessions.
- Support groups are there to support, nothing else. There shouldn't be any judgments or opinions.
- It values the privacy and confidentiality of the participants.

- It encourages people to open up, not force them to do so.
- It has a wholesome, inclusive atmosphere.
- Rules and regulations are clearly defined and explained to every newcomer.
- There is at least one cognitive-behavior therapy (CBT) qualified professional among the moderators, preferably an ERP therapist.
- Socializing is as important to them as providing OCD support.

Types of OCD Support Groups

A support group isn't always an association of professionals overseeing random people discussing several parts of different problems. Sometimes, it is focused on a particular area of a mental disorder instead of the entire disorder in general. Basically, there are three types of OCD support groups.

1. **Educational**: Groups that focus more on informing the members about OCD than diving into its emotional aspects are educational support groups. Sometimes, they are created primarily for research purposes, but they also help out the members.

2. **Focused:** These groups focus on a particular topic or a specific aspect of OCD. For instance, an ERP-focused group is for those people who have undergone ERP treatment. Others would probably not understand what the members are discussing.

3. **General OCD:** This group is more like a public forum. Any OCD-affected individual can attend and discuss anything related to their condition. The other members will provide feedback or share their own stories. These groups are often depicted in movies and TV shows.

You can find your nearest support group online. Alternatively, you can find support groups that are entirely based online. If your child is not ready to step out into the outside world yet, online groups are their best option. They include forums, chat groups, social media groups, video conferencing groups, etc.

Questions to Ask the Moderator

Before choosing the right group for your child, you need to ask the moderator or the founder of the support group the following questions.

- Are you accepting new members? Most OCD support groups don't charge anything, but it doesn't mean you can just march in and sit for the session. Many groups have a tight-knit setting of a select number of people. Always ask this question before considering that group.

- How many members do you have currently? Your child may not be comfortable with too many people around them yet. Select the group with the right number of members.

- What does a session look like? Ask the moderator to summarize its structure, from how it starts to how it concludes and everything in between.

- What are the qualifications of moderators or supervisors? Typically, the people who run the group need to have some form of qualification regarding OCD. Make sure that they have a CBT certification or at least some experience with cognitive therapy.

- Miscellaneous questions: Ask everything else that comes to mind about the support group, right from essentials like meet timings and duration to extras like the confidentiality agreements.

Building a Community for Continued Success

Were you unable to find the right support group for your child? Are there no support groups in or near your city? There is no need to worry. If you have opted for CBT therapy for your child, they may have already been in touch with other OCD-affected individuals. If not, then know that support groups aren't essential for OCD treatment; they are more of a side benefit. Nonetheless, if you are determined to find a support group for your child, consider building your own community.

If you know someone who is suffering or has suffered from OCD, you can reach out to them and find other people with the same affliction. It doesn't need to be someone who has OCD themselves. Their family member or friend could have it. If they are affected by OCD or its effects somehow, then you can include them in your group.

Start by narrating your and your child's journey to combat OCD, your struggles, and eventual triumph. Encourage your child and the other members to open up. Build a community of like-minded people to ensure the continued success of your child's triumph over OCD post-treatment.

Chapter Takeaways

During treatment, most of the work is done by your child and their therapist. But after treatment, you, as a parent, play a major role in the healthy functioning of your child's OCD-free life.

- Plan for tomorrow. Make your child aware of how normal life can be, including the good, the bad, the ups, and the downs.
- Encourage them to talk with you about their problems to maintain their OCD-free momentum.
- Prepare them well in advance for the struggles they may face while transitioning from childhood to adulthood.
- Find the perfect support group for them. If you can't find one, don't hesitate to create one.

Post-treatment, make sure that your child's progress graph shows a more or less upward trend. It's okay if it falls sometimes, but majorly, it needs to keep rising. And for that to happen, you need to keep your child motivated to celebrate even their smallest victories. It's time for you and your child to have some fun in the next chapter!

Conclusion

Living with OCD can be tough. It can bring a lot of challenges to your family, from sudden outbursts to behaviors that might seem unusual. Seeing your child suffer because of OCD can take a toll on your family's well-being, but you should know that it's not the end of the world. This book has provided many practical tips and techniques to improve both your child's life and your own.

OCD can be managed effectively. You have learned how to handle your child's symptoms through methods like Cognitive Behavioral Therapy (CBT), medication, and gentle guidance at home. With some adjustments, your lives will get back to normal, and you can reduce outbursts and disruptive behaviors by teaching your child more helpful ways to cope.

Children with OCD can sometimes act out in ways that affect their school performance, relationships, and emotional well-being. They might engage in behaviors like hair pulling, skin picking, or excessive hygiene routines. It's hard to see your child suffer, and many children with OCD experience constant anxiety, self-criticism, a sense of being different, and other mental health challenges.

However, there are ways to help your child overcome these feelings and behaviors, improving the quality of life for everyone involved, including yourself.

Your child can learn how to live a happy, well-adjusted life despite having OCD. It just takes teaching them the right coping skills. The result will be a stronger bond with your child and a reduction in the most challenging aspects of OCD. Your child will thrive as they realize that OCD is just a mental disorder, not reality, and they can control it with some effort.

In addition to therapy, it's essential to provide your child with a healthy, nurturing lifestyle. Things like a balanced diet, regular exercise, and proper sleep can all contribute to their mental well-being. Once you've established a foundation of physical well-being, you can start attending therapy sessions and practicing new coping skills both at home and in school. Life can go back to being relatively normal, and you don't need to feel like everything is hopeless or will always be difficult.

Just remember that your child's challenging behavior is not their fault. They're not seeking attention or trying to be difficult on purpose. It's also crucial to understand that their OCD is not your fault or a result of any parenting failures. OCD affects many people, and there are constructive ways to deal with it. See this as an opportunity for healing and growth that you and your child can undertake together.

References

(N.d.). Choosingtherapy.com. https://www.choosingtherapy.com/exposure-therapy-for-ocd/

"Life Will Be Okay" — Kathy's Story. (2015, July 7). OCD in Kids. https://kids.iocdf.org/for-kids/life-will-be-okay-kathys-story/

25 Tips for Succeeding in Your OCD Treatment. (2014, August 8). International OCD Foundation. https://iocdf.org/expert-opinions/25-tips-for-ocd-treatment/

4 steps for helping your child set effective goals. (n.d.). Big Life Journal. https://biglifejournal.com/blogs/blog/goal-setting-for-kids

Aakash. (2023, February 1). OCD anger attacks - how to manage their symptoms? Mantra Care. https://mantracare.org/ocd/related-conditions/ocd-anger-attacks/

AboutKidsHealth. (n.d.). Aboutkidshealth.Ca. https://www.aboutkidshealth.ca/article?contentid=287&language=english

Akyurek, G., Sahadet Sezer, K., Kaya, L., & Temucin, K. (2019). Stigma in Obsessive Compulsive Disorder. In N. Kocabaşoğlu & R. H. B. Çağlayan (Eds.), Anxiety Disorders - From Childhood to Adulthood. IntechOpen.

Alyssa. (2022, March 2). OCD coping methods. Banyan Treatment Center. https://www.banyantreatmentcenter.com/2022/03/02/ocd-coping-methods-to-try-boca-raton/

Bendriss, G., MacDonald, R., & McVeigh, C. (2023). Microbial reprogramming in obsessive–compulsive disorders: A review of gut–brain communication and emerging evidence. International Journal of Molecular Sciences, 24(15), 11978. https://doi.org/10.3390/ijms241511978

Bilodeau, K. (2021, October 1). Managing intrusive thoughts. Harvard Health. https://www.health.harvard.edu/mind-and-mood/managing-intrusive-thoughts

Brady, A. (2019, August 18). 4 advanced meditation techniques and tools to deepen your practice. Chopra. https://chopra.com/articles/4-advanced-meditation-techniques-and-tools-to-deepen-your-practice

Brownings, S., Hale, L., Simonds, L. M., & Jassi, A. (2023). Exploring the experiences and responses of siblings living with a brother or sister with obsessive compulsive disorder. Psychology and Psychotherapy, 96(2), 464–479. https://doi.org/10.1111/papt.12454

Cinzia Roccaforte, P. D. (2023, August 29). What happens to the family when your child has OCD? Anxiety Disorders and Universal Health Care; Anxiety.org. https://www.anxiety.org/pediatric-ocd-effects-family-functioning-treatments-fcbt-fit

Conley, M. (2022, March 28). 45 quotes that celebrate teamwork, hard work, and collaboration. HubSpot. https://blog.hubspot.com/marketing/teamwork-quotes

Contamination OCD: 13 strategies for maintaining motivation and momentum. (2018, November 15). Mysite. https://www.talk-feel-act.com/post/contamination-ocd-strategies-for-maintaining-motivation-and-momentum

Daze, G. (2019, November 25). 5 OCD treatment options you should consider. BrainsWay; BrainsWay - Noninvasive, Innovative Deep TMS Treatments. https://www.brainsway.com/knowledge-center/5-ocd-treatment-ideas-you-should-consider/

de Mathis, M. A., do Rosario, M. C., Diniz, J. B., Torres, A. R., Shavitt, R. G., Ferrão, Y. A., Fossaluza, V., de Bragança Pereira, C. A., & Miguel, E. C. (2008). Obsessive–compulsive disorder: Influence of age at onset on comorbidity patterns. European Psychiatry: The Journal of the Association of European Psychiatrists, 23(3), 187–194. https://doi.org/10.1016/j.eurpsy.2008.01.002

Dibdin, E. (2014, January 4). 9 ways to cope with intrusive thoughts. Psych Central. https://psychcentral.com/health/ways-to-let-go-of-stuck-thoughts

Ehmke, R. (2021, August 10). What if my child resists the treatment, or the therapist? Child Mind Institute. https://childmind.org/article/what-if-my-child-resists-the-treatment-or-the-therapist/

Emily Brown, M. P. H. (2022, December 6). Can OCD make you angry? Verywell Health. https://www.verywellhealth.com/ocd-and-anger-5498573

Ferguson, S. (2016, May 17). Strategies for OCD and time management. Psych Central. https://psychcentral.com/ocd/ocd-time-management

Fernandez, T. V., & Leckman, J. F. (2016). Prenatal and perinatal risk factors and the promise of birth cohort studies: Origins of obsessive-compulsive disorder. JAMA Psychiatry (Chicago, Ill.), 73(11), 1117. https://doi.org/10.1001/jamapsychiatry.2016.2092

Fleming, L., Tartakovsky, M., & MS. (2017, June 15). OCD and anger: Causes, treatment, and how to deal. Psych Central. https://psychcentral.com/ocd/ocd-and-rage

For parents: How to explain cancer treatment to your children - Dana-Farber cancer institute. (n.d.). Dana-farber.org. https://www.dana-farber.org/for-patients-and-families/care-and-treatment/support-services-and-amenities/family-connections/for-the-patient/how-to-explain-treatment/

Four ERP implementation case studies you can learn from. (n.d.). Erpfocus.com. https://www.erpfocus.com/erp-implementation-case-studies.html

Furman, B. (2019, May 22). Helping children to overcome OCD: 6 creative strategies for parents. Mad In America. https://www.madinamerica.com/2019/05/helping-children-overcome-ocd-six-creative-strategies-for-parents/

Grover, S., Painuly, N., Mattoo, S., & Gupta, N. (2011). Anger attacks in obsessive compulsive disorder. Industrial Psychiatry Journal, 20(2), 115. https://doi.org/10.4103/0972-6748.102501

Hardis, J. (2022, May 23). Setbacks in OCD recovery - Joanna hardis, LISW-S. Joanna Hardis, LISW-S. https://joannahardis.com/2022/05/22/setbacks-in-ocd-recovery/

Having a conversation with your child. (n.d.). Thinkuknow.co.uk. https://www.thinkuknow.co.uk/parents/articles/having-a-conversation-with-your-child/

Himelstein, C. (2021, January 5). So, your child is resisting therapy—here's what to do. Sunshine Child & Family Counseling, LLC. https://sunshinechildcounseling.com/so-your-child-is-resisting-therapy-heres-what-to-do/

How gut health impacts mental health: OCD, ADHD, etc. (2018, September 12). Viome. https://www.viome.com/blog/whos-really-control-how-your-gut-microbiome-impacts-your-mental-health

How OCD affects social interaction at school. (n.d.). Adaa.org. https://adaa.org/understanding-anxiety/ocd-at-school/how-ocd-affects-social-interaction

International OCD foundation. (2014, May 25). International OCD Foundation. https://iocdf.org/expert-opinions/expert-opinion-family-guidelines/

International OCD foundation. (2014, May 9). International OCD Foundation. https://iocdf.org/about-ocd/ocd-treatment/erp/

Jones, H. (2022, May 19). How can you find OCD support groups? Verywell Health. https://www.verywellhealth.com/ocd-support-groups-5220564

Kelly, O. (n.d.). How to Recognize Signs of OCD in Children. Verywell Mind. https://www.verywellmind.com/parenting-children-with-ocd-2510563

Kelly, O. (n.d.). Obsessive-Compulsive Disorder Diagnosis, Symptoms and Treatment. Verywell Mind. https://www.verywellmind.com/basics-of-ocd-2510510

Krebs, G., Bolhuis, K., Heyman, I., Mataix-Cols, D., Turner, C., & Stringaris, A. (2013). Temper outbursts in paediatric obsessive-compulsive disorder and their association with depressed mood and treatment outcome. Journal of Child Psychology and Psychiatry, and Allied Disciplines, 54(3), 313–322. https://doi.org/10.1111/j.1469-7610.2012.02605.x

Lifespan. (2008, May 15). Young children with OCD benefit from family-based treatment. Science Daily. https://www.sciencedaily.com/releases/2008/05/080515101348.htm

Made of Millions Foundation. (n.d.). How to talk to your child about OCD. Made of Millions Foundation. https://www.madeofmillions.com/articles/how-to-talk-to-your-child-about-their-ocd

Managing OCD in your household. (2015, July 7). OCD in Kids. https://kids.iocdf.org/for-parents/managing-ocd-in-your-household/

McLean news. (n.d.). Mcleanhospital.org. https://www.mcleanhospital.org/news/family-supports-young-ocd-researchers-discovering-ways-better-tailor-treatment

Menza, K. (2017, August 28). I lost 20 lbs on the anti-inflammatory diet — and fixed my skin forever. Delish. https://www.delish.com/food/a55110/anti-inflammatory-diet/

Miller, H. (2017, July 10). 7 Strategies to Cope With OCD. Family Psychiatry & Therapy. https://familypsychnj.com/2017/07/7-strategies-cope-ocd/

Obsessive compulsive disorder - family and friends. (n.d.). Gov.au. https://www.betterhealth.vic.gov.au/health/conditionsa

ndtreatments/obsessive-compulsive-disorder-family-and-friends

Obsessive compulsive disorder. (n.d.). Gov.au. https://www.betterhealth.vic.gov.au/health/conditionsandtreatments/obsessive-compulsive-disorder

Obsessive-compulsive disorder (OCD) What therapy can help with. (n.d.). Bacp.co.uk. https://www.bacp.co.uk/about-therapy/what-therapy-can-help-with/ocd/

Obsessive-compulsive disorder (OCD). (2020, March 11). Mayoclinic.org. https://www.mayoclinic.org/diseases-conditions/obsessive-compulsive-disorder/diagnosis-treatment/drc-20354438

Obsessive-compulsive disorder (OCD). (n.d.). Mayo Clinic. https://www.mayoclinic.org/diseases-conditions/obsessive-compulsive-disorder/symptoms-causes/syc-20354432

Obsessive-compulsive disorder. (n.d.). Kidshealth.org. https://kidshealth.org/en/parents/ocd.html

OCD: Some facts. (n.d.). Upenn.edu. https://www.med.upenn.edu/ctsa/forms_ocdfacts.html

Padam, B. (2014, March 23). How to recover from OCD. WikiHow. https://www.wikihow.com/Recover-from-OCD

Pfeiffer, T. (2017, October 16). This woman's journey of recovery from chronic inflammation will inspire you today. Prevention. https://www.prevention.com/health/a20498158/chronic-inflammation/

Quick guide to obsessive-compulsive disorder (OCD). (2021, July 30). Child Mind Institute.

https://childmind.org/guide/quick-guide-to-obsessive-compulsive-disorder-ocd/

Robertson, R. (2019, January 16). Health tip: The foods your brain craves.

Russell, M. (2021, March 25). OCD in children: Guidance for parents. They Are The Future. https://www.theyarethefuture.co.uk/ocd-in-children/

Sample Account. (2016, October 19). Clear expectations for kids. Focus on the Family. https://www.focusonthefamily.com/parenting/clear-expectations-for-kids/

Schuster, S. (2015, October 13). 17 Quotes That Prove OCD Is So Much More Than Being Neat. The Mighty. https://themighty.com/topic/obsessive-compulsive-disorder-ocd/what-ocd-feels-like/

Sharma, E., & Math, S. (2019). Course and outcome of obsessive–compulsive disorder. Indian Journal of Psychiatry, 61(7), 43. https://doi.org/10.4103/psychiatry.indianjpsychiatry_521_18

Signs & symptoms of pediatric OCD. (2015, July 8). OCD in Kids. https://kids.iocdf.org/professionals/md/pediatric-ocd/

Simkus, J. (2023, April 18). What is exposure and Response Prevention (ERP) therapy? Simply Psychology. https://www.simplypsychology.org/what-is-exposure-and-response-prevention-therapy.html

Singer, J. (2017, December 24). You've beaten OCD – now what? Psych Central. https://psychcentral.com/blog/youve-beaten-ocd-now-what

Smith, S. G., MS, & LPC. (2018, March 1). Setbacks can be... GOOD? Stacysmithcounseling. https://www.stacysmithcounseling.com/post/setbacks-can-be-good

Spiro, L., & Bubrick, J. (2016, February 2). The parents' role in OCD treatment. Child Mind Institute. https://childmind.org/article/kids-and-ocd-the-parents-role-in-treatment/

Spotting the signs: identifying and supporting pupils with OCD. (2019, March 28). Optimus Education. https://my.optimus-education.com/spotting-signs-identifying-and-supporting-pupils-ocd

Stevenson, D., & Keller, J. J. (2020). Coping Skills & Strategies for OCD. Impulsetherapy.com. https://impulsetherapy.com/coping-skills-strategies-for-ocd/

Study skills and OCD. (n.d.). Academic Skills Center. https://asc.calpoly.edu/ssl/studyskillsandocd

Symptoms - Obsessive compulsive disorder (OCD). (n.d.). Nhs.Uk. https://www.nhs.uk/mental-health/conditions/obsessive-compulsive-disorder-ocd/symptoms/

The brain-gut connection. (2021, November 1). Hopkinsmedicine.org. https://www.hopkinsmedicine.org/health/wellness-and-prevention/the-brain-gut-connection

The gut-brain connection. (2023, July 18). Harvard Health. https://www.health.harvard.edu/diseases-and-conditions/the-gut-brain-connection

The Obsessive outsiders. (n.d.). The Obsessive Outsiders. https://www.theobsessiveoutsiders.com/

Valentine, K. (2021, May 10). Can OCD make you angry? NOCD. https://www.treatmyocd.com/blog/can-ocd-make-you-angry-anger-management-fear

What causes obsessive compulsive disorder (OCD)? (2018, March 30). Beyond OCD. https://beyondocd.org/ocd-facts/what-causes-ocd

What is Different About OCD in Kids? (2015, July 7). OCD in Kids. https://kids.iocdf.org/what-is-ocd-kids/what-is-different-about-ocd-in-kids/

What is Exposure and Response Prevention (ERP)? (n.d.). Ocduk.org. https://www.ocduk.org/overcoming-ocd/accessing-ocd-treatment/exposure-response-prevention

Made in the USA
Las Vegas, NV
20 June 2024